Acknowledgements

There are too many people to thar' ... have been an integral and important part of my journey in every way, including th... I have it published. However, in bringing t... I am indebted to my son David for his many hours

This book is dedicated to the me

Memoirs of David John Claude Roper
Spring 2020
During the Coronavirus Pandemic COVID-19

Prologue
Journey Begins.

I was an unlikely person to become an antiques dealer. I was born in August 1943, the only child of Sergeant Claude Roper (later Company Sergeant Major) and Betty, a domestic assistant cook.

My father, being in the regular army since 1934, was often away, especially during the war years, so my mother had taken rooms in Willow Walk, Cambridge, a street near to midsummer common. This is the address shown on my birth certificate, but shortly after my birth my mother moved with me to occupy a house at Brampton Road. This was owned by her brother (my Uncle John) who was also in the army, the house being empty following the death of his first wife.

The house was quite close to the railway marshalling yards and Cambridge station, which was frequently bombed, so my granny - being concerned for our safety - persuaded mum to move to the relative safety of Grantchester, just outside Cambridge, to live with her parents.

It is interesting to note that following this, to keep the house occupied, mum's sister (my Aunt Daisy) moved to Brampton Road, and it was at this address where, 22 years later, I was to meet the love of my life Cathy, who moved there as a lodger. I remained in Grantchester until we married in 1966. I attended the small village school from the age of 4 to 11 when, in 1954, I became the first boy to pass the 11+ and go to grammar school.

Grantchester has become famous for the TV series "Grantchester" with Robson Green, but historically it is known for Rupert Brooke the poet, who lodged at the Old Vicarage, home in recent years to the equally famous Geoffrey Archer, author and politician. It was a wonderful place to be a boy, and somewhere I enjoyed returning to regularly up to and beyond the death of my father in 1995.

I think I disappointed my father by not going to university, but in those days my all-consuming passion was farming. I spent every moment possible at the local farm, run by Bob Vigus who was a very well-respected breeder of dairy shorthorn cattle, winning many prizes in the agricultural world. On one occasion, I was permitted to attend the Peterborough Show for two days with the stockman and his son, and allowed to lead one of his prize-winners round the show ring.

When I left school, my father was understandably determined that I would not go into the work of agriculture, himself having left the poverty of working on the land at Outwell when he joined the Army in 1934 aged 18.

And so it was that I left school in 1959 and went to work at the University of Cambridge Veterinary School, where I was to meet Jimmy, who became my mentor for the antique business. I was still working there when I met my soulmate Cathy in 1965. So, it is from the veterinary school where the journey properly begins, and where I will commence my story.

Chapter One
The Foundations.

'Find a job you enjoy doing, and you will never have to work a day in your life', said Mark Twain. This is the story of how I did this.

It is 2020 and I am forced by the Coronavirus lockdown to do nothing except be at home with my wife. This has afforded me time to reflect on my life and career in an ever-changing antiques business. This story will share some of the colourful characters, wonderful places, and fantastic pieces of furniture that my career as an antiques dealer has brought to me.

It is a social history of England, as well as a document of the ups and downs of starting and maintaining a small business - through the highs and lows, good times and recessions, trends, fads, and fashions of life, over seven decades.

I have never really been sure what triggered my passion for antiques - there is no history of antique dealing in my family. I was however always keen to buy and sell (rabbits, chickens, old bikes) whilst still at school.

I was also always looking for extra jobs; when I started as a paperboy delivering the evening paper in Grantchester, I was soon known for my willingness to take on additional jobs in other areas when another boy or girl was ill or on holiday. I did deliveries in the evenings, on Sundays, was on standby for mornings, and I collected the payments for the papers in cash from the Grantchester residents on a Saturday morning.

I also had a small shed as a workshop and, together with my friend Tony Smith, I undertook several jobs for a few shillings, repairing things etc. Our most ambitious project was making a bookcase for a villager, who I remember was delighted with it - but then he took at least two months to pay. An early lesson!

I left school in July 1959, and just after my 16th birthday in August I started work at Cambridge University School of Veterinary Medicine. I was directed there simply because, at my pre-leaving interview with school and the Youth Employment Officer, I expressed my love of animals and farming.

I was to remain there for ten years, just drifting along, working in various departments, obtaining on the way City and Guilds Laboratory Technicians Certificate Intermediate, followed by the Advanced Level in Microbiology. I also gained enrolment as an associate member of The Institute of Science and Technology (AIST), and associate member of the Royal Society for Health (MRSH). In addition to these qualifications, I took an A-level course in Zoology - normally a two-year course which I did in just one year.

One of the departments at the veterinary school was under Dr Allan Betts (later Professor Betts), who had interests outside the vet school and connections in commercial companies with an interest in Animal Health - in particular, Spillers Animal Food Manufacturers.

Dr Betts and Spillers together formed a company called SPF Pigs Ltd and purchased a small pig farm at Dry Drayton, just outside Cambridge and some three or four miles from the veterinary school. Once again, I was to get involved with extra part-time jobs.

These jobs were many, and varied, and one included early morning visits (before I went to my day job) to a commercial abattoir, where pigs were being delivered by caesarean section. I was an integral part of the operation team. In fact, I was filmed doing this for student teaching purposes. The piglets were subsequently hand-reared in sterile conditions by the girls back at the farm. The piglets were isolated completely from their mothers, so that there could be no chance of pathogenic infections to the baby piglets.

This was a commercial adaptation of research being carried out at the vet school, in order to establish pig herds that were free from virus pneumonia and other transmittable diseases. I also did weekend help at this farm, where I was to discover that there was an added bonus (apart from the money!) in that they employed two girls, who lived on the farm.

One day I was approached by Dr Betts who inquired, given my many interests, if I knew of anyone who could dismantle a large, corrugated iron building at an empty and disused abattoir in town, as their company had bought it and intended to re-erect it at the farm.

'Yes', I replied, 'I'll get The Gang together and do it.' Thus began one of my bigger projects. The job was formidable.

I put in a price, got the OK from Dr Betts, and began to enlist the help of a work colleague, Ray, with whom I had formed a friendship. He in turn enlisted his brother, who was always short of cash, and his brother's friend from work (they both worked at the caravan factory at Newmarket). The brother's friend, George, turned out to be a giant of a lad who wasn't afraid of anything, and he was a whizz with a hammer!!

As we all had full time jobs, it was agreed that we would have to do the job on a Sunday. We arrived at 6:30am on a bright sunny morning, only to discover that the yard was securely locked up as the company who owned the yard still kept their vans there. So, what to do? Too early to ring Dr Betts, and anyway we realised we didn't have his telephone number. 'No problem' says the big lad, 'we'll climb over the wall!'

Taking down a corrugated iron building is not a quiet job, and George with his hammer and crowbar soon got stuck in.

The trouble was that the yard was surrounded by streets of terraced houses with residents trying to enjoy a Sunday morning lie-in. At about 8:30am, Ray came over and nudged me. I couldn't hear what he was saying because Keith and his mate George, and their hammers, were hard at it - Bash! Bash! Bash! They also had their portable radio on at full blast. Ray pointed towards the brick wall which surrounded the yard on three sides – it was decorated with rows of police helmets! I think there were about thirty of them.

I eventually managed to get the lads to stop and turn off the radio. I can't remember what the inspector in charge of the posse said, but I think it was along the lines of 'Well now, what's going on here then?'

I think that he and his men thought they had uncovered another Gunpowder Plot, or something equally notorious, and that they surely would all get commendations for catching us in the act.

I was always very good at explanations, but this was a bit tricky. Questions like: 'If you've got permission to do this, then why don't you have a key?' – a good question. 'Why hadn't the boss checked with the owners?' and, 'had he told them we were going to do this on a Sunday?'

Ray, Keith, and George were anxious to get on, as we only had this one day to do the job. They had travelled in from Newmarket, and wanted to get it done. So they carried on banging, much to the annoyance of said inspector, and it was beginning to look like he was going to lock us all up. I had given him the name of Dr Betts as our contact, but I did not have his telephone number. These were, of course, pre-mobile days.

Eventually, the inspector found that one of the offices was unlocked so he went in. He used the telephone to contact the police station, who were able to trace Dr Betts' home phone number. Ray and "Our Gang" carried on bashing!!!!!

I could see the irate inspector talking intently to someone on the phone. Luckily Dr Betts was at home. I am sure he was delighted to have the police wake him from his Sunday morning lie-in! After about 10 minutes, Mr Inspector emerged from the office with a smile on his face. Our story had been confirmed, and he and the posse departed – but with words of warning about making a racket so early on a Sunday morning.

But that was not the end. We completed the job about 2:30pm and at 4pm the farm manager arrived to collect the corrugated sheets which, as he also did not have a key to the yard, had to be slid under the gates to be stacked onto a large trailer on the road outside.

We were only halfway loaded when along came a police patrol who were clearly unaware of the morning's events. 'Well now, what's going on here then?' and 'well then, why do you not have a key to the gates?' and so it went on. The lads carried on loading, and I explained everything AGAIN.

The next day when I saw Dr Betts, he was highly amused. He thought it was very funny, and we did get paid! This would have been around 1962 or 1963.

I worked with Ray for about three years – he had returned to the vet school after completing his National Service in the RAF. He lived at Newmarket, and travelled in by train as he did not drive. I took my driving test as soon as possible after reaching the age of 17, and offered to teach Ray to drive. I used the skills I had been taught by my instructor, who was an ex-police driving instructor. Certainly, it was all fresh in my memory.

One of the girls at work owned an Austin 7 Ruby which had been restored to a very high standard. She married the son of a very successful builder, who bought her a Porsche, and she sold her Austin Ruby to Ray for £100. Ray took up my offer to teach him to drive, and in return he allowed me to use this little car, which was great fun. I would go over to Newmarket every Saturday and collect him, and we drove all over the place in that little car.

He took his driving test and passed first time! And he then persuaded me to teach his brother Keith and, guess what? Keith also passed his driving test first time. We had lots of fun with that little gem of a car for the next couple of years.

Ray and I also embarked on a venture to keep poultry on an allotment which I had rented. The poultry department for research at the veterinary school had a large incubator and incubated large quantities of eggs from their own farm. They used the incubated eggs for research before hatching, and any eggs not required were simply disposed of.

We hit on the idea of relieving them of some of the eggs (but allowing them to hatch first) so hundreds of free chicks!! To accommodate them we needed a large shed, so we set about a plan to build one, using Ray's brother and his friend George as free labour in return for the driving lessons.

Keith and George obtained loads of offcuts of timber and hardboard from the caravan factory where they worked - free for the taking. With the purchase of a few posts, some netting and roofing felt, we set to work on it at weekends. George was at it with his hammer - banging in time to the pop music which was always on his portable radio while they worked.

It was remarkable how quickly it took shape and George kept us amused - he was a real character. When a large rat ran out past me, I shouted to George who was on the other side of our rapidly developing shed. He cooly waited for it, and killed it with one blow of his faithful hammer, and then carried on bashing at the nails without missing a beat of his favourite hit at the time: Glad All Over, by the Dave Clark Five.

We had a couple of hundred chicks for nothing, and when they matured and started laying, we quickly found willing customers for new laid eggs among our workmates.

Ray and I made quite a team.

Chapter Two
A Landmark.

1965 was a landmark year. I met my Cathy (always called Kathleen by her Irish family).

It was love at first sight... and we were married a year later in August 1966. We started married life with a table my mother gave us, and a brand-new bed we bought. We moved into a one-bedroom flat, which was the upstairs of a semi-detached house. Another couple occupied the downstairs. This was in Windsor Road Cambridge, which was convenient for both Cathy's work at the Shire Hall, and my place of work at the Veterinary School.

Then began the hunt for second-hand furniture. We quickly realised that, at that time, in a city full of students, clean used furniture was in short supply and visits to several second-hand shops yielded nothing. I think the seeds for our future antique dealing were planted then.

After about eight months we managed to buy our first house, at Linton, some 13 miles outside Cambridge, and a necessary commute so that we could afford a family house. It was a new build, and yes, we needed furniture. After more unproductive visits to second hand shops, we bought a new sofa-bed which we managed to buy outright, and a new dining suite on finance from the Co-Op. My Auntie Doreen donated her old stair carpet, and there we were - set up for life. It was sometime later in the year when the real revolution in our lives began.

I had formed a friendship at the Veterinary School with a Scotsman called James (Jimmy) Richardson, whose job was to make Model Visual Aids for the teaching staff. This was of course pre-computer days, and he was brilliant at his job.

We usually had our coffee break in the common room, and chatted about many aspects of life. He was very knowledgeable about a wide variety of topics, but the subject of antiques was never mentioned. Our favourite seats were at the end of the room, where there were double windows and a small balcony looking out over the fields beyond the veterinary hospital wing.

It was on one of these days, sitting in our favourite seats, enjoying the break, and musing about our likes and dislikes, when from nowhere I suddenly found myself saying 'You know what I fancy? Opening an antique shop', in a sort of spur-of-the-moment, no reason, idle chatter.

To this day I don't know where that came from, but Jimmy's reaction was equally unexpected, and I have to say life changing. I might have expected a few words about the wisdom of having a safe job, the benefits of security, or even a few wry comments about dreaming being ok but now you're married and a family started, keep your feet on the floor, or other similar remarks. Jimmy was, after all, a level-headed Scot!

But instead, looking straight at me and without hesitation, he said 'I could help you there.' He then went on to tell me that in his early working days he was a porter at Sotheby's in Glasgow. Jimmy was by this time in his late 50s, but he clearly had an impressive knowledge of antiques and the trade in general.

Tea breaks after that became even more interesting, with Jimmy's stories and anecdotes about his experiences within this prestigious auction house in Glasgow. I don't remember if he ever told me why he left there, or when and how he learnt his artistic craft, but he was very talented, and very clearly undervalued by the teaching staff at the veterinary school.

Fuelled now by my enthusiasm for doing deals, and Jimmy's encouragement, I started to talk to a few others about my ideas. One such colleague was a lady called Molly. I can't remember what her role was, but she was someone with whom I had occasionally worked. I casually mentioned one day that I was thinking of dealing in antiques and second-hand goods. Her reaction was as unexpected as Jimmy's had been. She informed me that she had some bits to dispose of which were her mothers, and she (Molly) would be glad to get rid of them and clear up some space.

She invited me to call in to see her on my way home from work. I sought a quick word with Jimmy before I left. His advice was 'Be fair, ask how much she wants, and go with your gut feeling.' I cannot recall exactly what was for sale but there were some books, candlesticks, crockery, and a brass stand.

'Fine,' I said. 'How much do you want?'
Molly's response was quick and decisive. 'Give me a couple of pounds' she said, 'I need them gone'.
'Two pounds?' I questioned.
'Yes, that's fine' she said, and proceeded to get the items off the shelf.

£2 was not much, but a week's wage for me at that time was only £15. It seemed a fair deal. I was on my way!!!

Chapter Three
The First Deal.

The day after my visit to Molly's house I went to work as usual, with my purchases in the car boot. At coffee break, Jimmy was anxious to find out how I had got on. 'I'll come and have a look at lunchtime' he said enthusiastically.

I was a little apprehensive as to what he would think of my first attempt at buying. Looking intently at my collection of random items, he quickly spotted the metal stand and asked if I knew what it was. I replied, with some anxiety, that I didn't. Jimmy explained that it was called a brass trivet and was used for standing the kettle on in the hearth. I will always remember his words.

'I'll be your first customer. How much is it?'
'Well,' I replied, 'I only paid £2 for the lot, so what do you think?'
Without further hesitation he said, 'I'll give you £5 for it.'

That first deal will always be remembered - a generous offer from the man who had already inspired me so much.

With the first deal done, I quickly moved on to disposing of the rest. The easiest items to sell were the books because, as our place of work was out of town, most of the staff stayed in the vet school for their lunch break and were happy to acquire something to read during lunch hour.

Some customers asked if I would like to buy some of their own books from them, as they had many at home that they had read. Thus began a very steady trade in books from the boot of the car, and my tea breaks became somewhat shorter as I built up a very healthy trade in books - selling at one shilling and buying back when they had read it for sixpence. Thus, doubling my money on a regular basis.

The veterinary school was my main employment, but since getting married I had started part-time work as a waiter at Selwyn College, which was not too far from the vet school, waiting on the students in the Dining Hall at the evening meal - thus giving me an additional income.

There were two "sittings" with a break of about half an hour between them, and this gave me another batch of customers for a "Good Read", plus the sale of a few bits and pieces to the other waiters. The first sitting was just for undergraduates, but for the second sitting there was "High Table" for College Fellows and visiting "Bigwigs" as they were known. I was very quickly promoted to serving at High Table for the second sitting, alongside my dad who had worked there part-time for several years.

This job was not without its hazards. For example, to my great horror, an overfilled cream jug spilled all over one of the "Bigwigs" very expensive dark suit as I passed it between two diners. The ensuing tension was quickly dispelled when one of the other diners quipped… 'the pigeons are flying well tonight!!' causing gales of laughter.

Apart from earning extra money, the great bonus of being a High Table waiter was that we got a meal after we had finished serving, therefore reducing our household budget. Derek Childerley, the butler who was in charge, was very good to me. He knew I was keen to earn, and gave me extra paid jobs such as private dinner parties whenever he could. I ate very well when on duty at the college. Subsequently, I went on to do conferences in vacation time, often doing breakfast, lunch, and supper. Getting fed three times a day whilst serving these meals was a huge boost to our home economy.

I didn't think of myself as an entrepreneur, it wasn't a word much used in those days, but I suppose I must have been because, within a short space of time, I found my services being requested from several other colleges: Pembroke, Kings, Queens, and Trinity (this was around the time that Prince Charles was up at Trinity College, but I never saw him).

One event which dad and I did a few times was at King's College on Christmas Eve, waiting at table for the Choir boys and their parents, following the traditional Carol Service from King's College Chapel which was, and still is, broadcast live every year. I seem to remember we were paid 15 shillings and a supper!

I don't recall when I first started to go to auctions, or how I managed to find time between my main job and part-time working, with two children under two years old at home - but somehow, I did.

There were two main auctions in Cambridge: Hammond's, run by Eric Hammond, and a bigger organisation - Catling, Brady and Bliss, for which Mr Bliss was the main auctioneer. Hammond's sale was on a Friday, and Catling Brady and Bliss was on a Tuesday. I started attending Hammond's auction on Fridays, using some days from my annual leave - which was considerable.

I don't actually remember the first time I bought anything from an auction. I don't remember if I was nervous, but I probably was. I found the other dealers, who were obviously old hands, quite friendly, but I was limited in what I could buy. I needed somewhere else to sell and needed more suitable transport than my car. But the "bug" had bitten! I needed to up my game!

Chapter Four
Bite the Bullet.

We had acquired a few bits of furniture for ourselves, cheap bits, which I had painted up. I was ahead of my time with this. I frequently painted only the frame of the carcass and restored the wood on the drawer fronts or door panels to their beautiful original finish.

As a result of my DIY activities, I often visited our local hardware shop and, over time, struck up a bit of a rapport with the owner. With no pre-plan, I remarked one day that I was looking to rent some storage. Did he know of anywhere? He inquired as to the purpose. 'I buy and sell a bit of furniture', I explained.

A little thought, and he said, 'I'll see what I can do, come and see me on Friday?' The shop itself was part of a large old property at the end of a row in Linton (Cambridgeshire) High Street, opposite the Co-Op shop and next to a pub, The Prince of Wales.

I'm not sure what I expected, but when I returned to see him, he invited me past the counter into the storeroom behind, through a corridor, and into what obviously had been the living quarters, now empty and unused.

The corridor led to a door opening onto the street with two rooms off, both quite large. He was prepared to rent me the two rooms, which had access directly to the street via the front door, which was right beside his shop front. He would block up the corridor to his shop and include the use of electric light for the price of £2 a week cash.

Mr Williams (the shop owner) clearly trusted me, as this arrangement meant that I could access his premises as there was only a flimsy barrier separating the rooms from his shop. 'Let me know' he said, and I went home to consult with Cathy. Having two very young children already, and another on the way, I'm sure this wasn't what she needed to hear! We also would need a van if we were to start buying larger amounts of furniture.

Now, much is joked about mothers-in-law, but I had the greatest of respect for mine, and at this time she was over from Belfast on a visit. She knew of our dabbling and was fortunately supportive and encouraging. She produced £40 saying 'Get a van!' In those days it was quite easy to find a second-hand vehicle for that sort of money. Cathy and I both protested as we knew she was not well off, but she insisted, so we took it.

Having told Mr Williams that we would take the rooms, we set about finding a van. There was a small garage in my home village of Grantchester which sold used cars, and there we spotted a Standard 10 van, which we bought for £45. The next step was to make use of it and buy some stock.

Several visits to Hammond's Auction Rooms produced an array of furniture, three-piece suites, wardrobes, chairs, and tables. Enough to fill the two rooms we had rented from Mr Williams. The van wasn't large, so occasionally I had to make two trips from Cambridge to Linton.

To lift heavy items Cathy would help me, even though she was pregnant at the time. We also enlisted the help of our friend Mike Swann, with whom we had formed a close friendship, and his wife Liz. Cathy had shared a flat with Liz in Cambridge, after moving from Brampton Road up until we were married.

The next hurdle was to try to sell the goods we had bought. It was decided to place an advertisement in the Cambridge Evening News classified adverts section "Furniture for Sale", as we had scoured these adverts ourselves when setting up home.

The advert read something like this:

wardrobe £3, dining table £5, three-piece suites £15, cupboard 15 shillings, plus other items. 123 High Street Linton, evenings only, after 7:30.

This was to enable me to get home from work and to be there for (we hoped) any interested parties. At about 7:15pm on the first day of the advert (we had placed it for three nights) I decided to walk the short distance from our house at Fincham's Close to the High Street, where the rooms were.

As I walked along the High Street (I remember it was dark) I could see a large group of people along the pavement outside the pub next to the hardware shop. I remember thinking that there must be some event going on at the pub, but as I drew nearer I could see that the queue was formed from outside the door to our rented rooms!

As I unlocked the door, people just flooded in; this was indeed a Defining Moment. I found myself not struggling to sell items, but deciding who to take money off first. There was little haggling, but I do remember one lady enquiring on the price of a sideboard, pulling a face and saying, 'It's not worth that.' I just pointed to all the people looking around and said, 'Well, someone will buy it.' And someone did!

I don't remember how people took their goods away, but they must have, because on that occasion I don't remember doing any deliveries. I think I endeared myself to the pub landlord that night, as the car park was full of cars belonging to our customers - many of whom were still there in the pub when I finally locked the door to the rooms about 9.30pm.

I cannot recall Cathy's reaction when I got home that night, but I do know we were both unable to take in what had just happened. With occasional help from Mike, we continued buying an array of goods from the two auction rooms - mostly three-piece suites, dining tables and chairs, etc, all of which we sold in the same way by advertising in the evening newspaper. We did sometimes have to deliver bigger items, a very pregnant Cathy willingly helping.

My notoriety as a dealer was by now well-known at the vet school. One of the young research assistants approached me one day to ask if I would buy some items from her mother. One of Cathy's brothers, Hugh, was staying with us at that time and the two of us set off one evening to this young lady's home in Shelford, a drive of about half an hour.

We arrived at this rather large house with a sweeping drive at about 7pm as arranged. My work colleague (I can't remember her name) greeted us, and introduced us to her mother, a charming lady who showed us the items she wished to sell. It was quite a lot, so I gave a price for each individual item, and it was accepted. I paid, and explained that we would need to do two trips, as it would not all fit in the van in one trip. We loaded the van and promised to return within the hour to collect the rest.

After delivering the first lot to our storage rooms, we triumphantly returned to the house and rang the bell. It was not our very pleasant lady who answered the door, but a middle-aged very grumpy looking male! Somewhat taken aback, I explained that we had come to collect the rest of the furniture. He glared at us and, without saying a word, stepped back and allowed us in. It was with some relief that I saw my colleague and her mother in the sitting room, because I had begun to think we had returned to the wrong house! As we proceeded to collect the remainder of our purchases, Mr Grump followed closely from room to room without uttering a single word. Anxious to make some sort of rapport with him, I remarked that it had turned very cold outside. He replied, 'Get the stuff, and get out.'

Hugh and I exchanged glances and silently completed the task. I managed to say 'thank you' as we exited the house before he abruptly banged the door shut. The entire time we had been in the house for this second collection he had spoken not a word, other than that very abrupt sentence. The two ladies, who must have heard, carried on watching television without a single word.

The journey back to unload was full of self-questioning. What had we done? Maybe he thought we had ripped them off, maybe he didn't want to part with it at all? All those questions. Maybe when I saw my colleague at work the next day she would explain, but she never mentioned it and was as pleasant and polite as she always was. She never indicated who that grumpy man was (I assumed it was her father) and she seemed quite content with our transaction.

I have often thought about that evening, and wondered what the miserable git would have done if we had happened to mention that my assistant that night was an IRA man sent over by my mother-in-law to keep him out of harm's way.

The items from that deal were all good quality and sold quickly. I continued to visit the two auction rooms in Cambridge, and was generally well received by the other dealers. One, Mr Cooper, whose family business in Newmarket Road had spanned several generations, offered not to bid against me where possible; a generous offer from a man who certainly did not need my help, but I was certainly glad of his.

Chapter Five
Progress.

The two auction rooms were situated quite close together just off Hills Road in Cambridge, which was the route I took daily to go home to Linton, a distance of 13 miles.

The van was quite small, so I frequently had to make two or more trips back with the goods bought. The logical next step was to acquire a larger van. Our friends Tony and Liz from Cambridge did not have a vehicle, so they bought our little Standard van, and we searched for a replacement.

This was found at Pound Hill Garage in Cambridge, which was situated at the Madingley Road junction, not far from the Vet School. A quick visit there brought our attention to a larger Bedford van. This was an ex-AA patrol van with column change gears and sliding doors, and it had been very well maintained. The asking price was £40. This, by today's prices, seems extremely cheap, but to put it in perspective I was earning £15 per week - so it represented three weeks wages.

It was a good buy. I quickly got used to the 3-speed column gear change and it was a dream to drive. On warm days, you could drive with the sliding driver's door open - but when you braked sharply the door would slam shut ferociously, so care was needed not to have your hand or foot in the way!

I graduated a little in my buying, occasionally looking at the Evening News classified advertisements for items. Our home in Linton was only five miles from Saffron Walden in Essex, where we often went to church on a Sunday evening. This was our nearest Catholic church, and to this day it is the smallest church I have ever seen.

One evening I read an advertisement for a Victorian chest of drawers at Saffron Walden. A quick telephone call confirmed that it was still available, so I thought it was worth a trip to view. I set off on a very hot summer evening, found the address, and was shown the chest of drawers in one of the bedrooms. It was an exceedingly clean, bow-fronted, Victorian mahogany chest of drawers, and it was in excellent condition. I cannot remember the exact price asked, but it was very reasonable. I was excited to buy it, but getting it down the stairs and into the back of the van was going to be a problem, as the elderly lady was alone and obviously unable to help.

I was determined to buy it and get it away before anybody else answered the advertisement. Somehow, by taking out the drawers, I managed to get it down the several flights of stairs and into the van. I remember the purchase so well because of the extreme heat, and I was exhausted! I stopped at a little pub on the outskirts of Saffron Walden and bought a drink, and I have never been so glad to get a cold drink as on that night.

We had often discussed my leaving the veterinary school. My heart wasn't really in being a university laboratory technician for the rest of my working life. I had frequently searched for a change of career to earn my living, as I didn't think it would be possible to keep my growing family solely from the income I made from furniture dealing. I had applied for several jobs in the commercial sector such as insurance, or selling medical or veterinary products, but had always been unsuccessful through a lack of commercial experience.

So, when I spotted an advertisement for a sales negotiator for a house builder - H C Janes of Luton, I decided to apply, using my success in selling second hand goods from scratch as an example of my ability to sell. I received an invitation to interview at the regional office in Long Melford, Suffolk, with the expectation that history would repeat itself. I set off with little hope that I would be successful. I had been in this situation before.

I was introduced to the regional manager who interviewed me, following a brief chat to a man who was, the manager explained, the housing estate developer. During the chat, which started off amicably enough, he suddenly barked at me:

'What makes you think you can sell our houses?'
I felt an immediate anger and sense of "déjà vu". Same old, same old!
Without hesitation I whipped back: 'If your houses are that good, they will sell themselves.'
He glared at me for a moment and then, getting up, said 'Just sit there for a minute' and left the room.

At that moment I was sure it was just another waste of time.

After what seemed like ages, he returned and called me into the manager's office. After just a few more brief questions, the regional manager said, 'We would like you to attend a second interview at Luton. Can you do that?' I was amazed that I wasn't shown the door so, 'yes' was the obvious answer.

Approximately two weeks later I found myself at the company headquarters in Luton, a large and impressive building, and was duly interviewed by the sales director accompanied by several others, including the regional manager who I had met previously. The discussion centred mainly around my success with the selling of second-hand goods. They seemed very impressed, and the interview went well.

A week later I received a job offer, but it was conditional on my giving up the second-hand business! So the very thing which had facilitated my success into the commercial world was to be sacrificed! Nevertheless, I accepted, because this job paid more money than the veterinary school and gave me the opportunity to do something more rewarding.

Any doubts I may have had were dispelled when good old Jimmy, my catalyst into the world of antiques, gave me this piece of advice: 'Working at the university there are three types of people - the physically disabled, the mentally disabled, and the bloody lazy!! You do not fit into any of these categories' he said. 'Myself,' he continued, 'I'm in the first category'.

In this, he was referring to his inability to maintain a sense of balance or stamina. For example, he was unable to ride a normal push bike. Because of his condition, Jimmy had always taken the bus to work, but we happened to pass by the top of his road on the way there, so a deal had been struck to pick him up in return for his bus fare, which helped us towards our costs. A win-win arrangement!

Whilst giving Jimmy his regular lift home one evening, he unexpectedly invited us into his home, rather than drop him at the top of his street as usual. 'There's something I want to show you' he said. That something turned out to be an amazing collection of Belleek China. He was aware that Cathy, being Irish, would know exactly what it was. Which she did.

Since then, whenever I hear mention of Belleek China, I think of my old friend Jimmy. Dear Jimmy, a more honest, kind, and wise man I have yet to meet.

Chapter Six
First Steps in the World of Commerce.

So it was that after 10 years of working at Cambridge University, I began a new career in the commercial world.

My stay at H C Janes was not to be a long one, but an important one on the path to being a full-time antique dealer which, in 1969 when I set out in the world of sales, was not something that I had considered a realistic possibility. However, as I was to discover, the antique world is not just a career but is a bit like farming, it's a way of life, an addiction. Something which, again like farming, is not achievable without the absolute and complete support of your life partner, and in this I have been extremely fortunate. Cathy has been not only my wife but my business partner, often my labourer, and without doubt my rock.

I could definitely sell houses, and did! My first target was to sell the last few houses on an almost completed site, before embarking on a new development for which I had sole responsibility. One opportunity I quickly spotted when I set out on my house selling career was that there was another business here, ripe for the taking. Insurance.

Most of the houses I sold were to first time buyers who were in need of insurance such as property, contents, and life cover. So, I quickly obtained an agency with the Royal Insurance Group, which was permitted easily in those pre-regulation days.

I was allocated an inspector from within the Royal Insurance Group, from whom I could obtain expert advice at any time. I only had to supply the leads and ask the questions. This proved a very lucrative extra income with very generous commissions, particularly on the first year of life insurances, which together with renewal commissions added up year on year.

I went on to receive a small cheque for insurance renewals for quite a few years. I later added car insurance to my portfolio, and extended my insurance activities to include friends, neighbours, and later workmates in my subsequent occupations.

Before commencing work on the new site development that I had been allocated, I was given several other tasks. One of these included trying to secure a new building site for the company by tender, and the site in question would be judged by the design of the development, rather than price.

The local council in Suffolk asked for designs that would be most suitable for the needs of the local population, and my task was to research the local housing stock and identify any needs. I identified a definite shortage of bungalows, and together with the design team we submitted a plan for a site in Sudbury with a high percentage of bungalows. The council approved and we won the tender to develop the site. The trouble was that although successful, that project did not earn me any commission!

Another interesting task was to promote the company by way of an exhibition of their housing projects at Sudbury Olde Thyme Rally. The theme was everything "Olde Worlde" with steam engines, traditional fairground attractions, steam-driven organs, threshing machines, etc. The purpose of the exhibition for our company was to promote their traditional building techniques. It was a two-day event, so it was decided that myself and one of the regional office secretarial staff, a young lady named Valerie, were to be in attendance on the second day, while another secretary and salesman covered the first day.

We were required to dress in period costume - Valerie in full length Victorian dress, complete with bonnet, and myself in a frock coat with tails and a top hat. The outfits were hired from a theatrical company, and Cathy starched the collar of a white shirt and ironed the corners down to form "wings" which were worn with a bow tie.

I collected Valerie from her home and we headed for the fair, but as we arrived at the exhibitors entrance we realised that the other couple who had attended the day before still had our passes, which we needed to obtain entrance. So, with the steward demanding to see the pass, I improvised. I mumbled that it was somewhere among all the paperwork and started to rummage through the glove box. Valerie just smiled and looked charmingly at the irate steward.

'It's in here somewhere' I muttered, and started rummaging through my briefcase. With every passing moment the length of the queue behind me was increasing. Finally, the exasperated steward capitulated and waved us through. Valerie kept on smiling.

She commented when we finally got through 'Typical salesman! Could charm anybody!' I took that as a complement. We had a good day, not hard work at all, and my antics at the gate circulated around the office the next day, to everybody's amusement.

When our new building site at Kedington, Haverhill (which was local to me being only twelve miles away, and therefore involved a lot less travelling time) was finally started, the housing market had slowed dramatically due to a huge hike in interest rates at that time.

The company was not concerned about this lull, they simply said it would pick up again, but I was frustrated. I worked full time including weekends on the site, and often during the summer I would even return in the evenings in a bid to catch any potential customers.

So, when one evening I spotted a man looking round, I pounced. He told me that he was looking for a bungalow for his mother. I gave him the full treatment, even offering to take them both to see a completed property on another site, as my site at that time did not have any completed bungalows yet.

By this time, it was clear that I was not going to let him go without a commitment. He said 'I'll come clean. I'm not a potential buyer. I'm actually a local estate agent doing a bit of research.'

A few days later, he came to see me again. 'I was extremely impressed with your sales technique' he told me. 'If you ever want a job, come and see me' and presented me with his business card, which read Neil Lanham Estate Agents, Haverhill.

This event was very significant when I look back. My career, and life, may well have developed in a very different but parallel way. When I did ring Mr Lanham, several weeks later, to our mutual disappointment it turned out that he had just taken on someone else. He had assumed that I was not thinking of leaving my current position with the building company H C Janes.

He did not feel that he could give back word to the person he had so recently employed, but he invited me to come and see him one evening anyway, which I did. We chatted for over an hour. He showed me some of the projects he had ongoing, including an antiques auction of period oak, which he held three times per year at Clare - a lovely little town about eight miles away. This was all very interesting and intriguing to me. We both realised that we could have worked well together, and to our mutual benefit. But it was not to be.

Fast forward a few months, I left H C Janes and got a job as a milkman with the Co-operative Society, so that I could return to dealing part-time. It was a means to an end. It wasn't bad money and I like being up early. Neil Lanham also got me to do some weekends for him as a sales advisor on a site at Haverhill, where he had the agency to sell on behalf of a small developer - just a few miles away from the site at Keddington where I had first met him.

In the meantime, my friend Mike Swann, who worked for an estate agency in Cambridge, used his contacts to find me an empty shop in Kingston Street Cambridge at a very modest rent of £2 per week.

With a small bank loan of £50, again arranged through one of Mike's contacts, I decided somewhat rashly to leave my job as a milkman at the Co-Op, and ventured into full-time dealing. When I had met the bank manager, he had observed that I was somewhat undercapitalised. A definite understatement. I struggled along for a few months, although I did have some success and met some interesting people.

One such person was Tom Sheridan, an Irishman who, when he first came into our shop, had the appearance of a tramp. He always wore a very old long overcoat. He had discovered our little shop, and it soon became apparent that he was very knowledgeable. His technique was one with which I have since become very familiar. He would come in and just look around (not go directly to the item which he had actually spotted the minute he walked in), looking first at all sorts of bits, before casually going over to "the spot" and enquiring casually 'How much is this?'

He never knocked me down in price, although I realise now that I was probably selling very cheaply just to turn stock over, but after purchasing the item he would impart quite a lot of knowledge about the piece. So, I learned quickly. Tom would call on average about twice a week, sometimes with his girlfriend who was much younger than him and very pleasant. Sometimes she would come alone, just to see if any new stock had arrived.

As I got to know them better, it transpired that Tom was a very wealthy man. He owned quite a few properties in Cambridge rented out to students, and he later confided that he owned a large hotel on the west coast of Ireland.

Whilst I was enjoying the work, we were short of money. We had two young children, Cathy was expecting our third, and our financial situation was very tight. My contact with Neil the estate agent revealed that he was not entirely happy with the young man that he had employed after I declined to leave Janes the builders. However, he didn't feel that he could do much about it, so he still couldn't offer me the job, which now I would have jumped at. The first couple of months of 1970 were tough, so I resolved to get another job as soon as our third baby was born.

I was buying my stock from adverts in the evening newspaper and from auctions. Fortunately, I secured several bargains and so managed to keep going. It was surprising how quickly I was accepted, as in those days it was mainly dealers who attended auctions. I recall one occasion when arriving at Catling's Tuesday sale, which started upstairs, and I was just a few minutes late. The sale had already started and as I reached the top of the stairs, I heard my name as the hammer went down.

I had bought two feather filled armchairs for twelve shillings and sixpence (sixty-two and a half pence in today's money) without even being present. The auctioneer Derek Bliss later explained 'I knew they were your thing and that you wouldn't be long before you arrived, so I didn't want you to miss out.' The same auctioneer, a couple of weeks later, knocked down a large quantity of white wood furniture, brand new, made so that you paint it yourself, for only £5 to me. There was so much that it almost filled the van. I sold them quickly and with good profit, thus surviving another week. The vendor of the white wood furniture was so annoyed about the price that he came to the shop to complain to me. I retorted 'No one else wanted them!' and referred him back to the auction rooms.

Another good sale where I got into trouble was a very good quality three-piece suite which I purchased from a private vendor. I got it for a good price by pretending that it was for myself. She later spotted the suite in the shop window and rang me to complain about misleading her. The moral here is that if you tell lies, you'll be found out. But I made good money and we lived for another week.

Our baby girl (Bernadette, our third child) was born on 12th March 1970, a little bit earlier than expected. The following day, I went to the Co-Op dairy where I had previously worked, and got a job to start straight away. This was a week before Easter, and it was a tremendous relief. The milk round I was allocated was based at Bishop's Stortford, some twenty miles away from Cambridge, so I had to journey thirteen miles from home in Linton to the dairy in Cambridge, pick up a milk float, and then travel a further twenty-plus miles before starting delivering. But it was a relief. At least I would have a regular wage again.

No sooner had I got used to this new job and started to plan how to combine it with my own business, the inevitable happened. That "Sliding Doors Moment" when my career in antiques may have taken a very different path. Neil Lanham, estate agent, rang me to say that his assistant had now left, and would I still like a job? I just felt so frustrated; after such a spell of great difficulty, I did not want to risk another change. It was just not meant to be. Twice now Neil and I had missed the opportunity to work together. Such is fate!

In later years, when I started to receive the Antiques Trade Gazette, I frequently read about Neil and his auctions at Clare. He went on to be a leading specialist in Period Oak furniture, achieving some record prices. The job he had offered me was selling property, but he knew of my interest in antiques, and as his reputation had grown who knows what my path would have been. I regard this as one of those situations which shaped our lives - where different decisions shape our future.

By now, 1970, we had three children, David aged two, Kevin aged one, and our newborn Bernadette, plus a mortgage, a job, and a shop which was thirteen miles from our home in Linton but just around the corner from the Co-Op dairy where I worked. So, we devised a plan.

The shop had living accommodation above, such as it was, just basic bare bedrooms and bare floors, a very basic toilet, a sparse "kitchen" (just a sink and a very old-fashioned gas cooker). There was no hot water, no heating, no washing machine, and this was the era of cloth nappies! But we lived there for three days a week, thus keeping the shop going but avoiding the travel. I don't know how Cathy managed with those basic facilities, three very young children, and a shop to look after. But for a few months at least, manage we did!

I carried on the job at the dairy, did a couple of different rounds, and after several months the manager asked if I would take on the job of relief roundsman / supervisor at the Haverhill depot, which was only about six miles from our home in Linton. A lot less travel and £2 a week extra, which represented an increase of about 10%. This was much needed at this point in our lives, and so I took it on.

The Haverhill depot was home to about six milk rounds, and the first one I did was delivering in and around Clare (the same little town where Neil held his specialist oak auctions), a lovely small town with beautiful countryside around it. Quite a bit of the round was in the rural area, including farms which were very isolated. This was in May 1971 and the weather was great, being out at 4am in such beautiful surroundings - I loved it. I can't remember at this point how long we carried on with the shop, but I did the holiday cover at Haverhill, and then there was another unexpected development which helped to map our path.

The foreman at the Cambridge depot, Ron, kept calling me back to the main depot, and was generally being an ass. Ron had a reputation for looking after all his cricketing chums. If there was a match on, Ron would make sure they either finished work early, or got the day off. This was almost unheard of at that time - everybody in the dairy industry worked seven days a week. One afternoon I went to see the assistant manager to clarify my position. I was supposed to be based at Haverhill, but Ron kept getting me back to Cambridge to help his mates. I went into the office prepared to do battle.

'What's the game with Ron?' I questioned, as soon as the door was closed behind me, expecting a bit of an argument.
His reply was just as quick. 'Don't worry about Ron. He's gone.'
'What do you mean he's gone?" I asked, somewhat taken aback.
'Left the area, run off with the landlord's wife from the Rose and Crown' (which was the local pub near the Sleaford Street depot).

Ron wasn't all bad - after all he did buy some insurance from me!

Thus began another chapter in my life. The manager offered me the foreman's job - there and then. I accepted.

And so began a period when I had a very responsible job, a bit of extra money, a few perks like free milk, but no time to advance the antique dealing. From a financial point of view, it was sensible to follow this career change, so for a period of about three years we did little actual dealing.

Chapter Seven
A Diversion.

My replacement at the Haverhill depot was obtained, and I started my new job at Sleaford Street Cambridge almost immediately. It was late September, and I was plunged in at the deep end - covering winter sickness, preparing for the Christmas rush, and reorganising several of the milk rounds which my predecessor Ron had set up for the convenience of his mates to give them an easy ride, rather than for efficiency and the smooth running of the daily deliveries.

There were sixty-three rounds in total, including those at Bishop's Stortford and Haverhill, so including relief roundsmen I had seventy-five men to organise. I am a great believer in that any experience you have during your working life, there is something to learn, something which you will be able to utilise at some point in a later situation. My skills of organising were severely tested in this role, but I believe I acquitted myself well. I never received any criticism from my direct boss, the assistant manager Doug Knights, who had been in the foreman's role at the dairy when my dad had worked there a decade or so earlier.

My duties included interviewing and hiring new staff, organising sick cover when the flu season put dozens of our roundsmen off sick, plus the ordering, packaging, and distribution of cream for our very busy Christmas period. Another (self-imposed) duty was to increase the volume of sales, and part of that was to motivate the roundsmen to sell extra products such as eggs, yoghurt, orange juice, etc.

I was supposed to have an assistant to enable me to have one day off per week. This was one of the perks that came with the foreman's job, as roundsmen worked seven days a week. Doug told me to pick someone to promote to assist me. The first person I chose was John Williams, with whom I had a good rapport, and we worked together for almost two years until he found the responsibility too much, and he went back to being a roundsman again.

I appointed Roger Moule as John's successor. Roger was one of the first members of staff that I had personally interviewed and hired. Together, we organised and improved rounds and delivery routes, we came up with a lot of incentives, and in general I really enjoyed the work.

It was tough on Cathy though. I seldom got my day off and did not get any extra pay for working it. Many times, when I was supposed to be on my day off, the phone would ring at 4am with a problem (usually someone not turning in for work) and off I would have to go. With young children this was very hard as I was not able to spend time with them. Had I remained in my position as a roundsman, I would have gone home as soon as I had finished my deliveries, usually mid-morning, but the foreman's position dictated that I was at work until around four or five in the afternoons, even if I had started at 4am. We employed students during holiday periods and they were a useful source of extra help at busy times - especially during the Christmas rush.

December 1971 - the Christmas preparations went well. I worked Christmas Eve night from midnight until 5am, enabling me to have the rest of Christmas Day off, and I was due to have Boxing Day off as well. At 4am on that Boxing Day morning, I received a phone call from the duty checker at the depot in Sleaford Street Cambridge, to say that one of the roundsmen at Bishop's Stortford depot had phoned in sick. Since we had no one else available I had to set off from Linton, and guess what? Yes, it was snowing!

I told Jack (the checker) to organise two of the student helpers and get a van ready. It was past 5am when I arrived at the Cambridge depot to pick up the van and helpers, leaving my assistant John to sort out any further problems. We set off to Bishop's Stortford, twenty miles away, in heavy snow.

By the time we arrived at the Bishop's Stortford sub-depot it was 7am. We started to load the milk onto the van and found the round book, but since we had no idea of the route, we had to consult an A-Z street directory to find out where to start.

It was midday before we had even got halfway round. We went back to the depot at about 1pm for a toilet break and a warmup. Fortunately, we had found a corner shop open and bought some pies to keep us going. By this time, the lorry bringing the milk for the *next* day's delivery had arrived, and so I formulated a plan.

Since we clearly were not going to finish before dark, I decided that, with the conditions being so bad and a long journey back to Cambridge when we finished, it would be better to use the milk that had just arrived to double up the deliveries to the remaining households on the round. When we reached the end, we could retrace our steps on the first part of the round and leave their next day delivery too, which would give my two helpers the next day off.

The helpers agreed with the plan, so when we reached a public telephone box, I called the Cambridge depot to update them.

We finally arrived back at the Cambridge depot at 8:30pm only to find that the yard and garage were all locked up. The night watchman was not even aware that we were still out. Worse still, when I finally arrived home around 10pm, no one had let Cathy know what was happening. I had left home at 4:30am that Boxing Day morning in heavy snow, and she had no idea where I was.

The next day, although the two helpers did get the day off, I was obliged to go in - but not until 10am, so at least I managed to have breakfast with the kids.

This was just one of the more "memorable" experiences that I had while doing that job, there were others, all of which taught me something!

During my time as foreman, I was sent on a very interesting two-day course at a very nice hotel in King's Lynn, during which we each had to give a talk about any interesting subject, either concerning work we had done, or hobbies that we enjoyed. The talks had to last at least 10 minutes, but preferably 20 minutes. It will be no surprise to anybody who knows me that mine lasted 40 minutes! It was very well received!

The topic I chose to talk about was my work with the pigs at the Veterinary School; another illustration of how every life experience reaps its own reward. One man gave a very interesting and informative talk on home decorating. I learnt a lot in that couple of days.

Later, in 1973, I decided to relinquish my role as foreman. In many ways I did enjoy the job, but the hours were too invasive of family time, and I had no time to pursue our shared interest in buying and selling. I opted to return to being a milk roundsman to give me more time to pursue these interests and spend more time helping at home. By now, we had four children, Stephen being born in November 1972. The management were unconcerned about me returning to roundsman duties. However, neither they, nor I, anticipated what was to happen next.

The procedure for loading the milk floats in the mornings produced a queue between 5am and 6am. This caused discontentment and a lot of grumbling among the men. They brought all their complaints to me because I was well known and had been their boss for the previous three years. One of their biggest gripes was the fact that, as Co-Op employees, they worked seven days a week, whereas Unigate operated a system which gave its staff a week off every six weeks.

I suggested that the remedy was to take their complaints to the Union. They did so, and an evening meeting was arranged. During the meeting it transpired that they did not have a shop steward to represent them in the dairy department.

I was busy chatting to someone and not taking too much notice of the fact they were asking for nominations. I heard someone say my name and before I could respond a voice shouted, 'I second that'. The union organiser asked for a show of hands, and within minutes I found myself elected as shop steward!!! I was stunned, but it seemed I didn't have much choice. Another new experience was born.

The management was shocked to say the least. They had assumed that with no shop steward in attendance, this attempt at a workers' rebellion would just fade away as it had done in the past. They knew me well enough to know that I would make changes. And I did.

I was summoned by management the next day when I returned from doing my round. I was assured by them that, as I would be required to attend meetings etc, they would pick the best relief roundsman to cover my delivery round whenever I was needed by the Union or staff, so that I would not have to work on those days. I would be present at every important meeting that was held, and any disciplinary meetings would also require my presence. I quickly learnt that I had a considerable amount of power but, to be quite candid, I was not that bothered.

The round allocated to me was semi-rural, in and around the region of Saffron Walden. I quickly improved sales and developed good relations with several customers. At around 7am each morning I made a delivery to the local hospital, and the kitchen manager always had a cup of tea and some toast waiting for me. Fabulous!

I canvassed several small shops and got them selling our milk. One of the shop owners was very interested in antiques, and he had a room devoted to old bottles which he had collected from "digs" around his area.

Another customer, only fifteen minutes from the end of the round, always had a cup of tea ready for me. When she saw me at the bottom of the road, the kettle went on. A good life! I even managed to sell her son some insurance.

My efforts as shop steward were not without some achievements. One of the most significant changes that I was able to implement was a "rota system" like that operated by Unigate Dairy - an achievement I feel justifiably proud of. Under this new system, each roundsman worked seven days a week for six weeks, was paid for six days, but on the seventh week they got a week off at the same pay.

To facilitate this system, additional staff had to be recruited and trained. This was quite an undertaking as it involved every additional person learning more than one round. I enjoyed this work as "Union Rep" and I became very popular with the men, much to the annoyance of the management, but things ran smoothly.

I was, however, still in pursuit of trading for myself.

I regularly read Daltons Weekly, a magazine which specialised in advertising businesses and property for sale throughout the UK. Also, there were several antique and second-hand shops in Saffron Walden where I did my milk deliveries, so I began to call into them frequently to browse (no one questioned a milk float parked on yellow lines!) The visits to these shops gave me further inspiration.

Whilst perusing the Daltons Weekly, we noticed that property in parts of the North of England such as Lancashire was considerably cheaper than in Cambridge, so our interest and speculation in that area began to grow.

The week prior to Easter 1974 I started one of my scheduled weeks off, beginning on the Sunday before Easter. Cathy was cooking our Sunday lunch and we began to talk about visiting the North-West, with Morecambe particularly in mind.

On the spur of the moment, we made a momentous decision. We would go "Up North" and have a look around. We very quickly packed up clothes and toys for the children, Cathy cut up the meat that she had just roasted and made sandwiches with it, put them in a tub, and with all the food we could muster we packed everything into the car - a Vauxhall Victor Estate with a huge boot.

By late Sunday afternoon we were heading off via Bedford and onto the M1 and then the M6. We drove through the night, the children sleeping in the car during the journey, and I got some shut eye by stopping at several service stations on route. We eventually got to Morecambe about breakfast time the next day.

I often wonder how the kids were able to behave so well, but I think they were excited by the whole adventure. David was only six, Kevin was five, Bernadette was four, and Stephen just over a year old.

On driving into Morecambe, we came to Regent Caravan Park and decided to seek one of the caravans to rent for a few days. Luckily the caravan park had just opened for Easter, and the owner happily agreed to rent us a large caravan for three nights, which we considered would be enough time to allow us to look around.

The children were as good as gold, enjoyed being in the great adventure, and loved being at the seaside. During the next three days we looked around several housing estates in and around Morecambe, and viewed a property which gazed across at Heysham power station! It was advertised as having an orchard, which in fact consisted of just three fruit trees. I often thought about that after we bought Hill View some years later, which had approximately thirty very old and established fruit trees, and really could be called an orchard.

During our tour of the area, we saw several housing estates by a local builder. We liked the design of the houses, but none of the actual site locations. I also visited a milk depot run by the Milk Marketing Board and inquired if I would be able to secure a job if I moved to the area. The manager's response was immediate: 'Can you start tomorrow?' So, it was confirmed that I could secure employment without any difficulty, which would be necessary to get a mortgage.

Our three days soon passed, and we had not found a suitable place to put down roots. On Maundy Thursday, we vacated our rented caravan and headed down the A6 towards Preston, where we had lunch. We then resumed our journey along the A6, stopping off at Leyland to buy Easter eggs for the children.

As we set off again to join the M6 at junction 28 in Leyland and resume our journey home, just within sight of the motorway junction we spotted a builder's sign advertising houses for sale with the slogan "last two remaining". This was the same builder whose houses we had liked in Morecambe, and we decided it was worth a quick look before we got on the motorway. We discovered that the small site was almost finished, and there was only one semi-detached house left. There was no sales office, so the site manager showed us around this house, and thus, within an hour, we had paid the deposit and bought the house.

Whilst the paperwork was being completed, we kept the children quiet by letting them eat their Easter eggs - all sitting in the big boot of our estate car. They thought they were in chocolate heaven! And we were rewarded with the pleasure of looking upon these four happy smiley chocolate-smeared children's faces, each one beaming back up at us.

By 4pm we were heading back towards Cambridge down the M6, and busy making plans to get our house at Linton on the market. An eventful few days indeed.

The next day, Good Friday, we set about decorating the smallest bedroom in our house, as this was the only room which we thought needed improving before marketing the house. Our next-door neighbour had previously sold her house, but then she had decided not to move and was withdrawing from the sale. When Judith, our neighbour, heard of our plans, she suggested that it might be very likely that her let-down buyer would be interested in our house.

The next day, Easter Saturday, I contacted the agent for our neighbour's property. They confirmed that this buyer was still urgently seeking a property in our location. Following a brief discussion to negotiate a reduced rate of commission, we agreed to place our property with them, and a viewing was arranged for Monday. The buyer concerned, who worked for a bank, already had a mortgage in place and no property to sell - therefore it was the perfect scenario. It was all agreed within just a few days. It was meant to be.

Back at work, I outlined my plans to the dairy manager. I think he was relieved. Getting rid of me as shop steward must have made his year! I was only obliged to give a week's notice, and this I would do as soon as we had a moving date. The dairy manager recommended Unigate Dairy as my prospective employer, so I decided to write to the Preston depot, and received a reply which assured me that there would be a job available.

As soon as I was in possession of a firm date for moving, I contacted Unigate again. An interview was arranged at Preston, so I travelled up north again and subsequently received a job offer. By the end of the second week of July 1974, we were on our way and installed in 16 Edinburgh Close Leyland, where we would live for the next seven years. By September, three of the children were enrolled at their new school, St. Catherine's in Leyland, and we were embarking on the next big chapter on the road to antique dealing.

Chapter Eight
Right Place - Right Time.

The beginning of our new life was not without its challenges. We moved in July at the start of the "July Fortnight" when almost everything and everywhere was closed down for two weeks for the annual holiday (followed, as I later learnt, by a week at the end of September). We had experienced nothing like this complete shut down in Cambridge; I had arranged to start work a week following the move, to allow us time to settle into our new home.

We were unable to obtain any of the things we needed for the new house such as items to connect the gas cooker, carpets, and all sorts. All the shops were closed for the fortnight, as were most of the other suppliers and tradesmen, so we couldn't procure any of the things or people we needed to get the house sorted. This was great "fun" as you can imagine with four small children.

When I did start work, I was not impressed with the round that I was given in Preston. I was not used to having to go out every Thursday and Friday evening to collect the money, nor did I like so many of the other northern practices with which we were so unfamiliar. Almost daily, when driving back home from work, I would think to myself, 'I'll stick to it for two years and then we'll go back'.

Over a period of a few months, we managed to get the house sorted and get settled in. The children started school, except Stephen, who was twenty months old. David, who was only six, struggled to settle at school at first. We couldn't understand why. He was bright, eager to learn, had loved going to his previous school, and had a happy outgoing nature. One day, after school, he asked this question. 'Mum, what does '**is it eck as like**' mean?' And we realised that he just could not understand the Lancashire idioms, or the accents of his classmates. The Lancashire dialect was a lot more pronounced back in those days, almost 50 years ago.

We shopped at the Co-Op supermarket in Leyland, and developed a casual friendship with the man on the fruit and veg counter. He was always chatting to the children, and it transpired that he and his wife were interested in antiques. He was later to become a regular customer in our early trading years at Leyland.

Cathy had discovered the local auction rooms, Warren and Wignalls, and made an early purchase of a modern four poster bed, which she thought was great. We attempted to look around some of the many antique shops which we had discovered in New Hall Lane in Preston - the main antique area which boasted a dozen or so established antique shops and it was growing. Most shops displayed a notice on the door which clearly stated: "Trade Only". It was hard to convince these hard-bitten dealers that, although you had a car full of children, you were trade. Most of them just threw us out!!!!!

There were two exceptions. One was Terry Stephenson, trading as Dee's Antiques, and another was Billy Cowell, trading as W. Cowell and Sons. Both were shortly to become very significant in our progress along the road to running our own very successful and long-standing antiques business.

Early in 1975, I transferred from Unigate at Preston to the Leyland depot. This saved a lot of travel time, and we could utilise this to our advantage. We had little cash to spare, but we started to visit Warren and Wignalls auction at Leyland and bought items, which we then sold to Terry or Billy. We then tried to advertise for items to buy in the Lancashire Evening Post, but this was relatively expensive. Little by little, we built up our knowledge and contacts, but it was slow progress.

When we decided to take the plunge and move "Up North" we had planned to get a boat or a caravan, so when we bought this particular house, which was on a corner plot with a good amount of space at the side, we made the decision to go ahead and buy a caravan.

One huge advantage of working at Unigate was the rota system, which by now was even more generous than it had been originally - working seven days a week for only three weeks and then we got the fourth week off. Having the caravan enabled us to take the children away often, and at very little cost. Furthermore, it offered us the chance to visit antique shops while we were away - Wales was only an hour away and Scotland a similar amount of time into the border areas.

Our first caravan trip was to Porthmadog in North Wales. We were destined to return there regularly over the next thirty-plus years, and enjoyed very many great family holidays there. Our first visit there was during the heatwave of 1976, when there was a water shortage even in Wet Wales!!! In spite of the fact that Stephen nearly drowned during our first visit to the beach, we all really enjoyed it, and we visited any antique shops we came across - gaining knowledge as we went.

It was around this time, while looking through the Lancashire Evening Post, that I came across an advert by a Preston firm of estate agents for a small shop to rent in the centre of Preston. It had previously been a hairdressers and was part of a building which housed the Christian Book Centre, owned by the Catholic Church which also had a small primary school nearby.

I arranged a viewing. It had a fairly large front showroom with a large shop window, a further showroom behind, a "back room" which would be very useful, as Cathy could spend any spare time waxing and refurbishing our furniture when not actually selling to customers, and it had a small kitchen and toilet. It was a bit rough, but nothing a lick paint wouldn't cure.

Most importantly, it was cheap. There was no formal lease to sign, and we could park in the yard behind. The rent was only £6 a week. This amount I could easily afford out of my wages, even if, at worst, we sold nothing. I did not debate long - we took it. A few days later, Cathy seemed apprehensive and asked me if I was worried about this very big step. Somehow, I was not. This was, after all, what we had moved up North to do - to get our own business going at last.

Insurance for the property was to prove the biggest hurdle. I went to the office of the Royal and Sun Alliance, as I had dealt with them as an agent when house selling. An inspector from the company came to visit the shop, and this is when I first met Alan Prescott-Casson, with whom I was to do much business in later years when he started his own business as an insurance broker. It transpired that antique dealers did not have a good record with insurance companies - the very words "antique dealing" seemed to conjure up visions of very dodgy people! However, Alan persevered, and we got cover – but with the exception of theft.

Since living at Leyland we had developed a friendship with our window cleaner, John Beasley. John was a good all-round DIY enthusiast who expressed his interest in learning more about the antiques. He offered to help with any jobs at the shop. He built glass shelves on wooden supports for the front window, and helped me to paint the shop front. The shop looked very well, and we set about stocking it. I had been experimenting with hand stripping furniture, as pine was very popular at this time. Before we left Cambridge, I had visited a large pine shop called City Road Pine, and that had inspired my interest in this aspect of the business.

We became frequent visitors to Warren and Wignalls auction and established ourselves as regular dealers. The saleroom at that time was situated near Leyland outdoor market (later this moved to the indoor market in Towngate), opposite to where Tesco supermarket now stands.

We made several useful contacts at the saleroom, including Derek and Madge Dalton. Derek was confined to a wheelchair following a motorcycle accident which left him paralyzed from the waist down. They set up the business following his accident and focused mainly on house clearances. I once asked them how they managed to do it, since Derek was unable to access stairs and give prices for the items upstairs. Madge explained that she would go upstairs and make a list, and if necessary, bring down (for example) a drawer from a chest of drawers so that Derek ascertained the age etc, and then they would give the prices from the list.

They were really quite successful, covering Parbold (where they lived) as well as Ormskirk and even Liverpool. At that time, English antiques were big business throughout the world, and Derek and Madge sold to the "shippers" but reserved any pine furniture for us. They had four children in their early teens, all of whom helped in the business, and I was able to buy quite a lot from them as time progressed.

We opened the shop on Fox Street Preston in 1975. I carried on working at Unigate and looking after Stephen during the daytime, while Cathy looked after the shop. One the first day of opening, Cathy went into the shop with some trepidation about what to expect. She returned, by bus, triumphant, and also a bit fearful, because she had the staggering amount of £90 in cash in her handbag. A fortune!!! We were on our way!!!!

Our very first customer had purchased, amongst other items, a washstand which needed to be delivered to the KFC takeaway shop at Blackburn Road, Samlesbury. The owners, Fred and his wife Jenny, were very enthusiastic about their purchase, and after the item had been put into place in its new home, we were treated to a huge family box of Kentucky Fried Chicken to take home. We rarely had takeaways, so this was a real treat and the children were delighted.

Fred and Jenny became regular customers. They were in Preston usually twice a week as Fred's brother had the KFC shop on Fishergate, just around the corner from our shop (this is the UKs first KFC, incidentally). Every time we made a delivery, we were given a huge supper to take home. We became firm friends, and the children enjoyed playing with their kids in their home behind the takeaway.

Our shop on Fox Street proved to be in a very good position. Winckley Square was nearby - the home of many solicitors and insurance offices. There was a steady flow of people walking up and down Fox Street. There were also two estate agents in the street, two jewellery shops, a music shop, among others, so together with the Christian book centre next door and the school, which was still open at that time, we had a regular footfall of customers, and we took money every day.

We were helped by the fact that most other antique shops in Preston would not open to the public, so we were selling a variety of collectibles as well as furniture. Cathy built up a good display of fans which were mounted on a wall and looked very impressive, plus ribbon plates which were popular at the time, a huge variety of ceramics, and of course stripped pine furniture - which would become our speciality.

An additional and unexpected bonus of this shop was that we built up a very steady stream of regular clients wishing to sell to us. These were mostly older retired people, and they would come to us when they had just received the rates or electricity or similar bills, and needed to raise the money to settle them. To Cathy it seemed very sad that they had to sell off their cherished antiques to pay their way. She dealt with these clients extremely fairly, and it was a win-win for both us and the clients. They achieved a good price for their items, and we had a continuous supply of stock which was "fresh to the market" as they say in antique lingo, and which is every dealer's dream.

We were indeed in the Right Place at the Right Time!

Chapter Nine
Trying Times.

The shop ticked along nicely. I continued to work at Unigate, and my regular week off every month was a great asset. As time went on, we were getting several regulars calling in, including a dealer from Lower Penwortham who dealt mainly in Victorian Dolls. She would come in almost every week buying ribbon plates and other antique china for her shop. We had made a speciality of early porcelain; she was delighted to have a constant supply of beautiful china for her shop, and we were glad of her custom.

Around this time, we heard about an antique fair at Park Hall, still in its infancy, based in the Banqueting Suite and trading on Sunday mornings. We decided to take a stall there. At this stage there were only about two dozen stall holders. We did steady trade, both selling and buying. I say "we", but as I worked three Sundays out of four, it was down to Cathy to stand the antique fair, taking the children with her.

At this time of our lives, Stephen, being the youngest, was not yet at school, so during the week Cathy would drop him off with me on my milk round before she went into the shop. She usually found me somewhere around Royal Avenue / Parkgate Drive (where we eventually moved in 2018). Stephen stayed with me until I finished doing my round, which was usually about an hour, and I then took him home on the crossbar of my bike. Eventually we were able to afford a car each, which made life so much easier.

It was a time of rapid development. We were buying more from Derek, and our forays out to other antique shops around Blackburn, Accrington, and other northern towns were producing a rich harvest, and this together with Warren and Wignalls meant we needed storage space.

Our friend John found us a small outbuilding to rent at Prospect House on Sandy Lane, Leyland, and we continued to use these premises for storage until we obtained the use of a barn at Ulnes Walton.

I had casually mentioned to a customer on the milk round (a farmer's wife, who's farm at that time was at the top of Slater Lane, Moss Side, Leyland) that I was looking for a building to work in and store furniture. A few days later she opened the door and enquired 'Could I come and see "himself" later?' I had not met Billy Gill before. He was a typical farmer, and an even more typical "Lancashire Lad". 'Wat thee want it fer?' he questioned. I explained. 'Foller me' he said.

We went about a mile down the road to a disused garden centre where the yard was strewn with scrap vehicles and farm machinery. There was a very large building with double doors, situated behind a house which fronted onto Ulnes Walton Lane, Leyland. It had a sound roof and floor, was extremely spacious and perfect for our needs.

I enquired, 'Does it have electricity?'
'It will.' came the curt reply.
The next question I asked was, 'How much?'
'Wat thee thinkin?' he threw back at me.
'I wasn't expecting to pay any less than a fiver a week.'

He turned on his heels and, without speaking, headed back towards the doors. I followed him outside in silence and bewilderment.

As he shut the doors, he flung over his shoulder 'Start next Monday Lad, al'reet'. The next moment he was on his tractor and gone! He was a man of few words, was Billy!

The £5 a week I offered may seem, in these days, a very small amount of money. To put it into perspective, this sum represented a considerable percentage of my weekly wage. It was clearly irresistible to a sharp-eyed no-nonsense hard-bitten farmer with a redundant building.

Billy had purchased this ex-garden centre, together with the house and buildings, after the previous owner had gone bankrupt. He farmed the few acres attached, but the yard and buildings had been unused for some time, other than to provide a dumping ground for all his surplus machinery etc.

The house was occupied by his granddaughter and a few years later, when the granddaughter moved on, we tried to buy the house from Billy. He proclaimed his willingness to sell but, despite this, all attempts and approaches from me were met with unwillingness to come to any agreement or even a price.

This wily and shrewd Lancashire farmer just could not commit to parting with the property. He was certainly not short of funds. His wife told me that their previous farm had been compulsory purchased in the 1930's by the government, prior to the war, to build a Royal Ordnance factory, becoming known simply as the ROF.

In later years, the ROF would be redeveloped into a huge new residential and business area called Buckshaw Village. It is interesting to note that our youngest son, Stephen, became a commercial property solicitor and he was heavily involved in the transfer and sale of that same land, from Royal Ordnance to the private companies who developed the Buckshaw Village project.

When I called at the farm for the milk money at the end of the week, I asked Mrs Gill if I was ok to go down to the barn on Monday, and what about paying for the first month? 'He will see you there' she replied. I took some furniture to the barn on the Monday afternoon, and I had barely been there five minutes when I heard the familiar chugg chugg of his old tractor. He greeted me as usual with 'Al reet lad' and his hand was out before I could get the twenty pound note out of my pocket. I asked, 'Is that all right?' 'Aye' he replied, showing me the power socket that he had rigged up from the adjacent building. 'Al reet!' he wheezed, and was gone.

I rented that barn for several years, and although we spent quite a lot of time working there, we saw no one except at the beginning of every month when, as if by magic, within ten minutes of my arrival I heard the chugg chugg of his tractor... and he appeared, took his £20, and was gone. He never asked for any increase in rent, and he never bothered me. A real character!

A few months later, his farm in Slater Lane was also compulsory purchased, and Mr and Mrs Gill, and son Tom, moved to another farm at Cocker Bar. I continued to deliver milk to the new farm.

During one of these times when I was at the new farm, Mrs Gill told me that this was actually the third time they had been bought out by compulsory purchase! At the start of the war when they had been moved from Whittle-le-Woods for the construction of the Ordinance Factory, their old farmhouse had remained empty and boarded up until many years later, when the developers of Buckshaw Village eventually renovated it and sold it.

Billy Gill's home and farmyard in Slater Lane were demolished for housing development. The farm at Cocker Bar remains, and I remember Mr and Mrs Gill with fondness. Mrs Gill was always kind, and Billy was one of life's characters. The use of the barn was an integral part of the progress of our business.

The development of our business continued, making new contacts through Park Hall, and becoming ever more confident in our buying. There were several regular customers to our shop in Fox Lane who were private collectors, and these formed a backbone for our business.

There were also the now many people who regularly called to sell items to us. This became a routine part of our new venture, with many of these sellers calling on the three-month cycle when their quarterly bills landed on their door mat. All in all, these sellers had become a good source of varied and interesting items, but because we were still on a learning curve we often had to make a wild guess as to what to offer.

We also established buying relationships with a couple of "knockers" who as the name suggests went "door knocking" all over the place looking for furniture. One was based in Preston, and another, who was based at Lancaster, frequently travelled around Scotland "knocking". He became a very valued and useful source of new stock for us. He became known to us as "Dave the Dealer" and his appearance gave the impression that he was a rogue... but he was far from it. We always found him very trustworthy and reliable, and anxious to do a fair deal.

On one very memorable occasion, Dave, when visiting us, spotted a piece of furniture which I had been storing. This was a very large, impressive, dark oak coffer. Dave, the ultimate dealer, was immediately interested in it.

'How Much?' was his instant question.
'It's not for sale' was my reply. 'I have been keeping that for when we move to our next house'.
'Everything is for sale - everything has its price', Dave smiled.
I was adamant… 'Not for sale. I've been keeping that for years.'

I loved that coffer. Cathy hated it. Dealer Dave offered me numerous exchanges for the coffer, including jewellery, but I was steadfast. 'NO, NO, NO'" and so it went on.

A few weeks later, Dealer Dave arrived at our house in a yellow MG Midget car, having acquired it in some deal or other. Cathy immediately fell in love with it.

'It can be yours' beamed Dealer Dave, 'I'll swop it for the oak coffer.'

And the deal was done. The upshot of it was that, after having some tea with us, I transported Dave and the large black chest back to his home in Lancaster in my car, and the bright yellow MG Midget remained at our front door.

Almost a year later Dave resurfaced, and on hearing that we were about to move house and needed cash, Dave traded the Midget back again for a van load of pine furniture - so he got his beloved yellow sports car back again.

We would lose touch with Dave periodically, and then he would resurface. Dave was always very pleasant to deal with, but he had two weaknesses: women and drink. At the last count he was at wife number five! I was never sure whether the women drove him to drink, or the drink drove him to women.

Everybody who knew Dave liked and respected him. Quite a few years after our last dealings with him, he called on us one Sunday afternoon, accompanied by a lady who he introduced to us as the daughter of wife number two. She explained that Dave had been asking for a while to revisit us, to talk about old times. He was clearly unwell, and although we passed on our phone number, we never did hear from him again.

Our success with the Fox Street shop had enabled us to exchange the old Vauxhall Victor for a newer Ford Cortina Estate. Only a couple of months after obtaining the Cortina, I spotted another Ford Cortina Estate at Leyland Garage. It had a very reasonable price tag of £995. This was cheap. When I made enquiries about the car, it had a high mileage but was known to the garage, it had been owned locally and represented very good value, particularly as it was the Deluxe model with a bigger engine. It also had a tow bar - useful for our caravan. I decided to buy it.

This demonstrated just how much we had progressed with our business. I was able to buy without any hesitation and this enabled us to have a car each, making the logistics of balancing our shop, buying trips, and transporting four children to and from school, scouts, etc. much simpler, and life a lot easier.

Soon after acquiring our second car, we ventured on our first buying trip to Scotland - with the caravan. We stayed in the Border Regions for the week, visited several shops, and discovered a very amicable dealer in Lockerbie. We were able to buy a considerable quantity of antique fans, ribbon plates, and other "smalls", filling the boxes under the seating in the caravan to capacity. On our return, we quickly found willing buyers for our spoils, both in the shop and at the antique fair at Park Hall.

The owner of one of the estate agents in Fox Street, Tony Holdsworth, had visited our shop on several occasions, showing great interest and making general enquiries about our stock, eventually culminating in a request for a trade price for four chests of drawers. They were, he explained, for his wife's boutique fashion shop which was based in Leyland. This was quite an exciting moment, but we could not, and did not, realise at that time just how significant this was to be!

Meantime, there was to be another event which was a major contributing factor to our future path.

My time at Unigate was not particularly enjoyable, but I endeavoured to make the best of it. There were regular sales promotions of goods such as chickens, bacon, cordial, juice, bread, etc. I was one of the top salesmen, always in the top three and winning many rewards including vouchers for John Lewis, which proved very useful when buying Christmas presents for the children.

The depot manager at Leyland, Albert, was very laid back and easy to get on with, but then we got a new assistant manager, George, who clearly had been Hitler's Apprentice and was a sarcastic so-and-so. My first encounter with George was when I had a severe infection in my hand which prevented me from lifting the full crates of milk. I should have gone off sick, but Albert asked me to come in to work and assured me that the milk float would be loaded up for me.

Shortly after leaving the depot, three of the crates slipped off the float, smashing all over the road. This was before 6am. Fortunately, a resident heard the noise and came out with a bin and brushes to help me clear it all up. It transpired that the centre crates on the loaded milk float were not properly aligned. As I had not loaded the van, the fault was not mine. I had to call the depot for replacement milk, which Albert brought out to me, and promised that someone would come and help me finish the round… but nobody did.

On my return to the depot, after a very painful and difficult four hours delivering, I was informed by George that I would be charged for the lost milk – sixty pints!!! (You can imagine the amount of glass that was strewn all over the road). I maintained that this was not my fault or responsibility as I had not loaded the float, and furthermore I had come into work that day to oblige - rather than taking it off sick. George was adamant that I had to pay, so I handed in the rounds book and informed him that I would not be back to work until they agreed to fund the mishap. No sooner had I arrived home than Albert rang me and agreed that it was not my fault, that they would not be charging me, and would I please go into work the next day.

I did so, but the urge to leave the job and instead work full-time for myself was now even greater.

The situation at Unigate was to become even more fraught, and events which were out of my control were to make a significant change of direction inevitable.

One by one, the four children succumbed to measles - an unpleasant experience for them, but they were soon over it. Stephen was the last to get it and was quite poorly - this was during my regular rest week off Unigate, and therefore I was at home. I was able to look after him and this enabled Cathy to carry on at the shop, securing during that week the order for the four chests of drawers from Mr Holdsworth.

As the end of that week approached, I developed a rash on my neck so severe that I felt it necessary to make an appointment to see our GP, Dr Raven, as I also felt very unwell. Dr Raven, rather dismissively, said that it was caused by my scarf, and actually told me that he thought I just wanted to take time off work to help with "them kiddies" (he knew that they had all had the measles). I was indignant, but grateful for a sick note as I really did feel unwell.

This was on Friday afternoon and by Sunday I was really ill. I could not get out of bed, and had a severe rash all over my body. Cathy was so extremely concerned that she called out Dr Raven (you could get a doctor to do home and out of hours visits in those days!). He came, and apologised profusely - yes this was measles, and it was serious in adults. I was 34. He immediately signed me off work for a further four weeks.

I was extremely unwell, feverish, and delirious. The order for the four chests of drawers had to be delivered that week to Mr Holdsworth, but our new friend John quickly volunteered to help Cathy deliver them.

These two events (my illness, and the order for the chests of drawers) were to be a turning point in the path that we were to follow.

When I was able to return to work after 5 weeks, I was to discover the venom that can exude from people when they make judgements of others based on how they choose to see it, rather than on the true facts.

Following normal procedure, the Saturday before I was due to return to work on Sunday, I called at the home of my supervisor, Ray, to collect the rounds book and be updated with any changes to the round which may have occurred while I'd been off. This was normally an amicable chat - usually we each invited the other into our homes, as was the case when he would come to mine.

This particular Saturday the rain was continuous. It was clear that I was not going to be invited in, so instead I spent fifteen minutes or so on the doorstep while he explained the changes from the comfort of his hallway, while I got wetter and wetter on the doorstep. It was abundantly clear to me that being off sick had caused considerable resentment, as the others would have had to work their rest weeks, and even though they would have been financially compensated for it, they were not happy.

The general view was that when their children got measles, they were barely ill - so why was Roper off for five weeks?

When I returned to the dairy the next morning, no one, and I mean No One! spoke to me. It was quite clear that this was how things would stay for some time. But things were about to get worse. After finishing collecting the cash on that Thursday evening, I began to feel unwell. By the time I went into work on Friday morning, I could hardly lift the crates of milk. George made some sarcastic remark to me, to which I replied, 'If I feel any worse tomorrow, I will not be in.'

He exploded!!! 'You've only just bloody well come back' was his very angry response.

When I got back home that morning after work I felt very ill indeed. I managed to get an appointment at the doctors that afternoon. This time I saw a new doctor, a lady doctor. She was very definite that I had pleurisy, which she said was a complication that could occur as a result of having measles as an adult, especially if I'd got a cold. Which I did - following my soaking at Ray's house the previous Saturday. I was given antibiotics, together with the warning that I would always have a weak chest which would affect me more as I grew older. I was signed off work for another four weeks.

Clearly, this was going to cause further aggravation at Unigate!!

Being so poorly meant that I was also unable to do anything to help Cathy with the antiques business either. I was glad when I was finally well enough to return to work. Once I was out delivering on the round and dealing only with the customers, I was able to ignore the silence of my so-called work "mates".

Tony Holdsworth had taken delivery of the four chests while I was off sick, and still popped into the shop occasionally. One day, Cathy came home with a request from him for a price for about twelve mixed items of stripped pine, to be delivered to Stamford in Lincolnshire. We were excited, but also a bit apprehensive! This was a big step for us, and we had to think about the logistics of getting the delivery in place.

When we mentioned this to our dealer friend Derek Doulton, he offered to lend us his trailer to make the delivery, which solved our problem. My friend "Big Mark" offered to take the day off work and come with me. Mark was another new friend we had made since taking on the shop, and had been helping me a few evenings most weeks. We christened him Big Mark owing to his height of 6ft 6!

All that remained was to work out a price for what, to date, was our biggest job yet. I made a list of various items of furniture: chests, boxes, a wardrobe etc, a selection totalling twelve items for a price of £700. A fortune to us at that time. Cathy passed on the price to him, and we waited.

We continued making sales, both in the shop and at Park Hall, but I knew I needed some more volume and regularity if I was ever to venture into full-time dealing. We had, after all, tried when we were in Cambridge but lacked capital, and I didn't want to risk failure again. I had to keep working at Unigate until the time was right. We had negotiated an overdraft and a business account with the Midland Bank at Leyland when we took on the shop. We had also engaged an accountant in Leyland - so we were poised, but not quite ready.

This big order from Mr Holdsworth was vital. But would we get it? And where would it lead us? Our overdraft was only a few hundred pounds, but it had given us enough to stock the shop. Selling £700 worth of stock to one person would be a big boost. We started to prepare several items towards the order in anticipation... and we waited.

A few days later, a very strange incident occurred whilst delivering the milk for Unigate, which further increased my resolve to seek self-employment.

One morning before 7am, while delivering in Fox Lane Leyland, I returned to the milk float to find that the vehicle was at a crazy angle. One of the back wheels had dropped into the road, up to the axle, and was firmly stuck. Apparently, workmen had been laying pipes down under the road, backfilling and tarmacking the surface as they went. Clearly, they had not compacted this section thoroughly, and the surface had given way under the weight of the vehicle and the milk crates, most of which were still full.

I had to leg it to the nearest phone, which was on Leyland Lane (no mobiles then!) and try to explain what had happened to a bemused manager.

It was a full hour later when Albert and the yard man arrived with a spare milk float. They couldn't believe what they saw, but they simply got back into Albert's little van, and left me with this spare milk float and the job of having to transfer the entire load on my own. What would have been only ten minutes work between three of us, took me over half an hour on my own, adding to the hour that I had already lost.

Timing of delivery is vital on a milk round, and being so late I was forced to run for the rest of the round in an endeavour to make up some time. It was becoming very apparent to me that the time to tell them where to stick the job was fast approaching.

That week we got the breakthrough that we were waiting for. Mr Holdsworth gave the go-ahead for the dozen items of stripped pine - for delivery as soon as we could manage it.

Confidence boosted. Exactly what was required at this crucial moment.

Chapter 10
The Next Big Step.

The delivery to Stamford, Lincolnshire was arranged for when I had my next week off work.

Big Mark had booked the day off work, and we loaded the trailer that Derek had loaned us the night before - parking it in the barn at Ulnes Walton. The trailer was an open one, so we had to cover it up with a plastic sheet in case of rain - fervently hoping that it would be a fine day for the journey.

Mark arrived at our house at 6.30am and we set off promptly, collected the trailer, and headed for the M61 at Chorley, and onward to the M62. This was 1978, and the motorways were not as busy as they are today, but there was still a degree of anxiety as the wind caused the sheet covering our precious furniture to flap about constantly and alarmingly.

Our objective that day was to safely deliver this (for us) large order - and get our money. I had not actually met Tony in person at this stage, and knew very little about him! But we focused on the fact that he had already bought four chests of drawers, and was now (hopefully) buying twelve more items.

We could not have known at this point how significant this contact would turn out to be.

All the way down, Mark and I were debating about what to do if, when unloaded, he rejected any, or did not pay us.

The delivery address given to us was a house in Ryhall, just outside Stamford. Apparently, Tony had just recently moved in. The property, when we arrived, was a large and impressive Elizabethan house in the countryside, a beautiful place with a large gravel drive. It was with great relief that we had arrived safely. We drove in and parked up outside the door.

We were met not by Tony, but by another man who said that he was Tony's business partner. This was unexpected. He also informed us that the delivery address was not at the house, but at a property in the centre of Stamford.

We managed, with some difficulty, to turn the trailer around and followed this man approximately five miles into the centre of Stamford. The destination turned out to be a large period building, now empty, which had previously been a hotel.

We were confused because we had assumed the furniture had been for Tony's new house. Tony's business partner explained that he and Tony had set up a company to purchase and develop interesting properties. However, they had now decided to use this ex-hotel as an experiment in retailing antique pine furniture.

We were shown into the large entrance lobby. There was a spacious, stunning room off to the right, which had been the ballroom, and on the opposite side of the lobby was the dining room, which was equally vast and imposing. It was immediately obvious why they had decided on this location for their new venture into antique pine. It was in the centre of this beautiful historic town, and the imposing frontage was directly onto the street which created an instant "shop window" for the pine furniture in the setting of the glorious ballroom.

The potential for considerable footfall was obvious. I began to see a much larger opportunity here.

But still, our new contact was very vague, and then there was the issue that he wasn't Tony - who Cathy had got to know in previous dealings! Mark and I were getting more and more concerned about whether we would get paid, or not.

We were directed to unload the furniture into the ballroom. It didn't take long to unload the twelve pieces and set them out… and what had looked like a mountain on the trailer melted into the room, and looked lost.

Tony's partner, who's name turned out to be Duncan, watched without comment as we attempted to display the furniture to look impressive. Mark and I stood back, with a mixture of relief and anxiety. Mark asked Duncan if everything was satisfactory. After a few moments of brief inspection, he replied that it was fine, and immediately produced a chequebook.

He asked if £700 was the correct amount, and we both nodded. I put the cheque in my wallet, and we were off.

We followed the one-way system back to the A1 with a sense of immense relief. As we settled down on the journey home, we discussed how lost those few pieces looked in the vast space of the ballroom, and pondered the likelihood of selling them any more.

The next day saw me pay in the cheque with some anxiety, but we need not have worried. The cheque cleared, and we had made our biggest sale to date. What next? We could only speculate.

The little shop in Fox Street continued to make sales every day. Fred, our first customer, and his wife Jenny were regulars, together with several local dealers who had discovered us, and of course Billy Cowell, who at this stage was looking for "shipping furniture". When we got anything in this line we rang him, and he came and bought directly from our garage at home.

I continued for a short while to work for Unigate Dairies. I felt that it was time to take that big step to full-time dealing, but I was still concerned as I did not want to repeat the same mistake I had before. So, I had an idea for a "back-up plan".

There were a considerable number of private milkmen in our area at that time. Quite a few of them bought their milk from Unigate, and as such they visited the depot yard daily and knew me quite well. I decided to approach each of them to offer my services as a relief man if they ever needed any time off. I knew this was an area of difficulty for those self-employed dairymen.

In the meantime, Tony Holdsworth had come into the shop again, told Cathy that he had been happy with the pine we had delivered, and may well want more. Tantalisingly, we did not see him again for several weeks. As we later learned, this was the time when he was moving to the house in Lincolnshire, and parting from his wife.

My decision to leave Unigate's employ was hastened by Cathy hurting her feet whilst helping me to move a chest of drawers in the barn. I handed my notice in, and enacted my plan to approach the self-employed dairymen. This was very well received by them all. Indeed, one of them, Norman Yates, immediately booked me for a week to allow him to go on holiday, and offered me terms that were very favourable.

The events of the last weekend of my employment with Unigate gave my determination to work for myself a boost which I could not have envisaged.

George, the Hun, announced on my final Friday that he would be coming with me when collecting the customers' milk money, so that he could verify that each account was correct, and balances due were to be agreed with each and every customer. This was not normal procedure and was a huge insult. Once again, this was simply due to George's own vindictive behaviour, because in fact a week's wages and holiday pay were kept in hand by the company to guard against any discrepancy.

I informed him that he had left it a bit late, since I had collected over half the accounts on the previous (Thursday) evening. He replied that we would go back to all those customers to verify the accounts. I told him that he would be more than welcome to do that… but he would be doing it alone. I would not be going with him. George backed off immediately and did not suggest again that he would accompany me on Friday either.

My final Saturday arrived, and as usual I had young David with me, then aged about ten. Even at that young age he was a great help to me with the deliveries. George informed me that he would be accompanying me on the round that day, but that David had to go home. At that point I handed him the rounds book, and said 'If David goes home, I go home too'. The tone of my reply made it absolutely clear that I meant what I said - after all, I had nothing to lose. A very disgruntled George relented - he clearly did not relish doing the delivery round on his own.

Within an hour of setting off, George was full of praise for David's ability as a rounds boy, and had mellowed to the extent that, when we passed a little corner shop, he gave young David some cash to treat himself! What a turnaround!!!! By the end of the deliveries that day, George had become almost human, and was chatting away to David.

These attempts to insult me on the last few days of employment strengthened my resolve that I would never work for anybody again. My determination to succeed at working for myself was resolute. Freed from the shackles of employment, I was able to inject all my energy and enthusiasm into our own business.

The shop sales were steady. Cathy had built up a reputation for the items that she specialised in, such as small collectables, antique pottery and plates, and especially Victorian and Edwardian fans. She had many loyal customers who called regularly. We also sold an array of similar items at the Sunday antique fair at Park Hall.

Les, the greengrocer from the Co-Op who had become a friend, was also a regular buyer of ribbon plates, which his wife collected, and young David and I regularly took our new acquisitions to his home for them to look through at their leisure. They always bought something, and always treated David with nice biscuits and chocolate bars.

While this was all positive, it was apparent that to make a living we needed to sell furniture in bulk, and for that we needed trade buyers. Most of the antique furniture trade at that time was in "shipping goods" such as oak and mahogany tables, mirror-back sideboards, bureaus, chairs etc. The margins in this area were slim, as all these goods were traded in bulk for the overseas market. Any of these which we bought, either through our loyal shop customers or by advertising for house clearances, were consigned to our dealer friend, Billy Cowell.

But what of Tony Holdsworth? He had, after all, been our biggest customer so far. We had not seen him for several weeks. We needed to develop the stripped pine side of our business as it was possible to obtain good margins in that area. The extra profit came from the value we added by the physical work we put in: removing the old paint and then waxing and polishing the lovely exposed old pine wood. Mark and I had become very skilful at this.

I decided to ring Tony. By now, I knew that he had moved into the house at Ryhall, near Stamford. With considerable trepidation, after exchanging the usual pleasantries, I enquired what he had thought of the stock we had previously delivered. He replied, 'It was all fine. I could do with some more. When can you come back down?' Having established that our prices would be in the same range as before, he placed an order for a mixed load of about thirty items!!!!

We were on our way!

Chapter 11
Expansion.

It was "all-hands-on-deck" as Mark and I frantically processed a selection of furniture, working down at the barn until 10pm most nights.

Mark later told me that he often popped into the chippy on his way home, and wondered why he got such strange looks from the other customers. One night, before he got into the shower, he happened to look in the mirror. Sanding the furniture produced copious amounts of sawdust, and this was lodged in his eyebrows and covered his hair and face. With his huge height to add to the illusion - he looked like the Abominable Snowman!

I decided that using the borrowed trailer and sheeting up against the weather would not be a practical option this time. We decided to hire a Luton van, and so began what was to become a long association with Avesco, a local family-run hire company with depots in Preston, Wigan, and Blackpool.

And so, we delivered to the old hotel in Stamford for the second time. This time Tony was there, and more about his plans was revealed. He indicated to us that his intention was to buy more pine from us. This was of course very encouraging.

This was now a time of rapid development for our business. Our network of contacts developed apace, one of which was brought about by Mark's father-in-law, who still called into our shop in Fox Street. He had been instrumental in introducing us to Bri-Wax polish, which he had discovered during a visit to a pine shop in Skipton - Primrose Antiques.

Primrose Antiques also had a large caustic dipping operation (to remove the paint from the antique pine, revealing its natural wood state) in nearby Steeton, on the road to Keithley. Dipping pine in caustic was something that we had heard of, but we had no means of utilizing this as a method of stripping ourselves. The knowledge of this facility at Primrose Antiques was something we would use in the future.

Another contact we established was Mick Walsh, at Darwin. Mick stripped pine by hand, as we did, and he employed about five people. Stripping by hand was very labour intensive.

Some time earlier, we had earned extra money doing work for Billy Cowell a couple of nights a week, using this hand stripping method to process some of Billy's own furniture. Billy rented the top floor of the Preston Antique Centre, in New Hall Lane, owned by the Allison family. This was prior to Mark working with me, so I was assisted by my friend John. It was a vast space, with hundreds of items of antique furniture. We were given a small office to use as a workshop.

We would start about 7pm, and Billy would lock us in to the top floor until about 10pm for security reasons. Billy was punctual about returning at 10pm, so we were always cleared up and waiting. One evening, he was late. It got to 10.15pm, then 10.30... and no sign of him. Remember there were no mobile phones. We were locked in, so by 11pm we were getting worried. We wandered through to his office, which fortunately was unlocked, and were able to access the phone there to ring his home. His wife was still up, but Billy had gone to bed, and she had no idea that we were there. After locking us in that evening, Billy had gone to play snooker and then he completely forgot about us, went home, and straight to bed.

He arrived about fifteen minutes later to rescue us, full of apologies, paid us, let us out… but the drama did not end there. We were glad to get fresh air, made our way to our car in the pitch darkness, and proceeded to follow Billy's car as he headed out of the yard towards the exit onto New Hall Lane. As we turned the bend in the yard towards the gate, Billy was at a standstill a few yards ahead... the exit being blocked by a police car!!!! He did all the talking. Someone had spotted his car driving into the yard at such a late hour and alerted the police.

We continued working for Billy off and on for a few months, until he called a halt because he was having difficulty in getting payment from customers in the USA. Something which, as time went on, I heard about more often from different dealers.

Now that I had left Unigate, I was anticipating how my new contact with Tony would develop. I turned my thoughts towards a quicker way of stripping. The polishing was already quicker with the use of the BriWax. We had previously used varnish which took time to dry, and didn't quite get the right look that I had seen elsewhere.

We had made the second trip to Stamford and had been assured by Tony that he would call when, or indeed if, he wanted any further deliveries. We need not have been worried. Less than three weeks after this second delivery, he called to say that he had sold most of it, and how soon could we come down with some more?

This was the turning point.

Meanwhile I had been doing relief for Norman's milk round, and also for Ken Smith. They both employed young milk lads before school, and so it was not difficult for me to implement this "insurance policy" and continue the work on furniture restoration. Although this backup plan was no longer necessary thanks to our bulk orders, I was able to keep my word, do the relief rounds, and save the money earned.

The sales of stripped pine at Stamford took off like a rocket.

Tony named the business "Handsome Pine" and managed everything in a very professional manner. None of us could have predicted just how successfully this experiment of his would grow and expand.

January 1978 saw us take delivery of a brand-new Ford Granada Estate. We traded-in both Ford Cortinas as there had been some issues with each of them, but they had served their purpose.

New vehicle registrations at that time took effect from the 1st of January each year, and Leyland garage was arranging collections from 10am and all through the day. The car was purchased purely for practical purposes, but if we had done it to annoy the neighbours at Edinburgh Close, then we were successful. Things were already strained, as our immediate neighbours had stopped speaking to us since we had bought the caravan and managed to acquire a car each. So, with the arrival of a brand-new prestige car, the proverbial really hit the fan.

There had been many heated exchanges with our immediate neighbour, who objected to my coming home with furniture on the roof rack of the car which, in her opinion, was bringing down the tone of the neighbourhood, even though it was always only briefly on the drive on route to our storage premises.

As a result of our obvious success, there was considerable resentment among many of the neighbours, inflamed no doubt by the malice of this adjacent neighbour. However, this only spurred us on to work even harder, thus ensuring that our goal of moving to a bigger home with more space for our growing family would be achieved.

There was one notable exception to the hostility in Edinburgh Close, and that was Gaye Jerstice. Gaye was a young widow with two children, and we regularly looked after her daughter who was about the same age as our daughter, Bernadette (both aged five at this time), so that Gaye was able to continue in her full-time role as a social worker. We remained in touch with Gaye for many years until her death in 2019.

There was a very interesting "house call" arranged for us by Gaye, to a client who was having to give up his home in New Longton to go into long term care. I went to visit the elderly gentleman, accompanied by Gaye. Social Services had been unable to trace any relatives, and in all the time that Gaye had been involved with his care, there had never been anyone who called or visited him.

On arrival at the house, Gaye was somewhat surprised to see a car on the drive. When we entered, we found a youngish man who introduced himself as a nephew, and he was also a solicitor. He proceeded to vet any offers I made for the items to be sold. I had no problem with this, as all offers were a genuine appraisal of what I considered the items to be worth.

When it came to a 1930's bedroom suite (in immaculate condition it must be said) I offered £30 pounds, knowing that I could get £35 for this suite from any of the dealers who shipped to the USA. The nephew said he would get it transported to auction, as he thought it was worth much more.

When viewing the next sale at Warren and Wignalls in Leyland, I spotted this suite lotted up for sale that afternoon. The nephew later appeared in the saleroom, and after a friendly greeting he stood beside me as the item came up before the auctioneer. The hammer fell at exactly £30 - I was vindicated! I think he was rather embarrassed, but I commented that he had been right to follow his conscience. Secretly I felt rather satisfied with myself, knowing that he had commission and transport to pay out of the proceeds.

Subsequently I did quite well with what I had purchased from the house, and Gaye later told me that the old gentleman was greatly relieved to get it all sorted, and he knew that I had paid him a fair price for all his beloved belongings.

Progress in our business continued.

We worked hard and for long hours, and there were many occasions when we found ourselves having to work late into the night in the rented barn - polishing furniture, or loading for delivery, with all four children asleep in the cab of the van. It was a busy life, but with the caravan allowing us to escape now and then to our favourite destination of Porthmadog in North Wales, we made sure that the children also enjoyed this period of intense activity.

Chapter 12
Moving with the Big Boys.

It was with considerable speed that we found ourselves being accepted by the "big boys" who inhabited the antiques area of New Hall Lane, Preston.

Several of these dealers made regular calls to the shop in Fox Street, as well as our regular private customers. Since we were still learning, I'm sure that we bought and sold many things at bargain prices. We would always try to pay what a seller asked, or if they did not know, we would offer what we considered to be a fair price. Local dealers soon learned that we had fresh goods on a regular basis, and that we only put on a modest profit.

At this point in time, we took on a lady to work in the shop - Wyn Hughes. Her husband held a very senior post at Lancashire County Council, but he hated his job. Wyn was a frequent caller at the shop and was a staunch supporter of Dr Barnardo's charity. She would call regularly and offer us items to buy, which she was selling on behalf of the charity (few charity shops existed in those days). She was very interested in everything about the shop, and mentioned one day that she would like to work in an antiques shop. We were very busy, and Cathy had her hands full with four young children, working in the shop, doing Sunday fairs, and helping with polishing and waxing the furniture - so it was decided that we would offer Wyn a job. This was a great help to us, especially as Wyn was also happy to sand and polish furniture in the back room of the shop in between serving customers, and she was excellent in both capacities.

Wyn was to remain with us for about four years, up until we left the Fox Street shop. We have stayed in touch with her to this day with exchange of Christmas cards, and Cathy met up with her again in 2019.

Our success meant that we needed more space, and as I have previously mentioned, we dealt with Terry Stephenson who had a large shop on New Hall Lane, trading as Dee's Antiques, and he also had a warehouse at Lostock Hall.

I knew that "The Lane" was the place to be, and started to investigate the possibility of getting a shop there. Any shop that became available was hotly sought after and was usually snapped up within a few hours of being advertised. In conversation with Terry, he revealed to us that he had decided to rent out the upstairs floor of his shop. We jumped at the chance. We were lucky. The next day we discovered that another dealer had been chasing it, so we were fortunate indeed.

We were, by now, getting our furniture stripped at Primrose Antiques near Skipton. We had followed Big Mark's father-in-law's advice, and had been over to the shop in Skipton and then to the works at Steeton to investigate the caustic dipping process. We had recently acquired a trailer and were able, with this and our roof rack on the car, to transport large numbers of items to Steeton to be stripped there.

It was on a trip there, to collect the items they had stripped and drop off some more, that we first met the owner, Dave Bovingdon. It was a hive of activity, and I took little notice when this hippy-looking guy came over and started to assist with the unloading, chatting as he did so about where I was from, and the general nature of my business. I told him that I had been before, and dealt with Andrew. 'Well, now you are dealing with me, I'm the boss', he replied with a grin.

It quickly became apparent that we would get on very well. I became, as it turned out, a good and regular customer. Dave was an excellent man to deal with, and was always fair. He had a valuable source of stock and knowledge, and an efficient pine stripping operation in place.

In later years, Dave told me that I had become one of his best customers. Not the biggest by any means, but a regular weekly visitor - who paid. Many of his bigger customers took weeks to pay after the shipment, particularly French dealers, causing him considerable cash flow problems. Following the first couple of deliveries to Handsome Pine in Stamford, things accelerated considerably, and this required sourcing an ever-increasing amount of painted pine for stripping.

We were regular buyers of such stock at Warren and Wignalls saleroom, plus any pine obtained by the Dalton's in their house clearances, and from several other dealers who were glad to move pine from house clearances for cash. One such dealer was a young man I met at the saleroom, Paul Norris, who with his dad frequented Warren and Wignalls and did lots of house clearances in the Wigan area. Paul usually had his brother with him, Frank, who was obviously disabled, with some sort of brain damage. Paul later told me that this was caused at birth. I was full of admiration for the dedication which Paul showed towards his brother, taking him out as he did, and trying to give him something to keep him interested and occupy his days.

Over forty years later - I still see Paul, and he still supports his brother and his dad, who is now in his 80s.

With an increasing supply of the Victorian (and older) painted furniture, and the expansion of our sales - not only through our new contact at Stamford, but also with an expanding number of private sales through our shop - it was now very much a matter of getting furniture stripped. This was a lot quicker and easier using the dipping technique of Dave Bovingdon at Primrose antiques to remove the old paint.

The furniture had to be waxed and polished after stripping, and for this we enlisted the help of young David and Kevin, and a few of their friends. Most Saturdays there were about five of them beavering away. There were often minor repairs to be done on the furniture, and these were mostly carried out by our friend John Beesley.

Handsome Pine, down at the old hotel in Stamford, was selling at an unbelievable rate. Tony started by saying come down every four weeks, but was soon ringing us after a couple of weeks and asking how soon could we come back - and could we bring a larger quantity? This was progress indeed.

To effect this, we regularly hired a huge removal van, the largest I could drive on my licence. Mark and I were also finishing items as fast as we could. Mark worked about four nights a week, and I was at it every day. This was in addition to our boys and friends working at the weekends, they were all young and to their credit did a superb job of polishing these Victorian pieces of furniture.

We moved into the large upstairs rooms at Dee's Antiques (Terry Stephenson's shop on New Hall Lane) and that required an instant supply of ready-finished pine, so we sought to buy some ready finished items from Dave at Primrose Antiques. I was surprised that his prices were reasonable enough for me to purchase, but as I later learnt, cash flow was a big issue for Dave. Since I always paid straight away, and was usually spending £1,000 or more every week for stripping work and purchases of "ready for sale items", every trip to Dave's became a two-way buying and selling operation.

Our outlet at Terry's shop introduced us to the export market. At this time the USA were not great buyers of pine as they were mostly preferring Victorian oak and mahogany, but there were still several regular American dealers, and the French and Dutch market was very good for the sale of pine.

These times had to be experienced to fully understand the sheer quantity and demand for antiques, and the domestic trade for stripped pine was still increasing. It was "The Thing to Have" for young couples, and it also appealed to older people wanting the "In Vogue" look. And we were there at the right time!

Our shop assistant, Wyn, more or less ran the little shop in Fox Street, but she was not keen on the thought of moving to New Hall Lane - although at that time it was not being considered as an alternative, we were just using our outlet at Terry's shop to access the export market. We did not need to spend much time at Terry's shop, as there was always someone there to do the selling for us. It was just a useful extension to our business at Fox Street and our rapidly expanding outlet with Handsome Pine at Stamford.

We had only been renting the space at Terry's for about four months when we arrived at his shop one morning to be informed by Terry that the owner of shop opposite, which at that time sold new pine furniture, had placed a notice in the window at 9am that morning - advertising the shop to let. Terry knew that we were looking for a more permanent base of our own. But by the time we had arrived, this shop had already been taken - by none other than Billy Cowell, who, by 9:30am, had taken up the option of the lease on the premises.

Billy had a large warehouse on the top floor of the mill as I have already mentioned. His technique to operate this was to drive up and down either side of New Hall Lane first thing every morning, cherry picking any new stock that other dealers had brought in overnight. In doing so, he had spotted the "To Let" sign in this shop, been to see the owner, and signed for it.

It was an established fact that anyone who had a lease of a property in that area at that time could demand "Key Money", and would probably get as much as £500 cash. There were no flies on Billy! He knew that he would make money even if he didn't keep the shop for himself - and all of this by 9:30am.

I learnt a lot from dealers such as Billy. He once told me that he made most of his profit from those early morning sweeps, by being the first along New Hall Lane scouting for stock. This was a time when there were many terraced streets being cleared in towns like Preston, and residents were being moved into newly built accommodation. Every such house in these mill towns yielded Victorian furniture, as most people decided to buy modern for their new homes. Billy told me 'You make your profit when you buy it - buy it right and your profit is guaranteed.'

So it was, we spent the rest of that morning grumbling about the fact that we had missed the chance of a good shop in a good location. We were still at Terry's when Billy came in, probably just after lunch when he was doing his second sweep of the day along "The Lane".

We had, of course, been dealing with Billy for a while. I had sold him quite a lot of shipping furniture which we had acquired from various sources, and I'm sure he had benefited from many good bargains out of us.

I greeted him with 'You Jammy Devil!'
'What's up?' was his reply.
'We've been searching for a shop for months - and you nipped in and nicked it.'

I was smiling, so he knew it was just banter.
His reply was as unexpected as it was event changing.

'Well, you can have it if you want. Just give me some key money.'
I thought he was joking.
'No - it's yours if you want it.'
'How much?' asked Cathy.
'You can have it for £250' was his reply.

Cathy and I had a brief chat, but we didn't really have to think about it. Cathy was convinced that it would make a great showcase for our business, and so we decided that we would take it. The biggest boost to our journey took place that day!!!!

Once again, we were in the right place at the right time.

Chapter 13

134/136 New Hall Lane Preston.

This was the address of the property where our name was to become firmly established in the antiques trade.

Having agreed to give Billy the key money (which, given the demand for such a good-sized shop in the middle of the lane, was a very reasonable ask) he directed us to meet with the owner, an Indian gentleman who ran a clothing shop just a little further along the lane. He sold a variety of very reasonably priced children's clothes, and Cathy later bought many of the children's clothes there, including school uniforms. We were to have a very good relationship with Mr Cazoogie, who was a truly honourable gentleman.

We met with his solicitors in Lune Street Preston, and we had strict instructions from Billy that I was to stick to the story that he had told Mr Cazoogie, which was that I was his brother-in-law. We later found out that this was indeed the reason that Billy had taken the shop, but his real brother-in-law, who had expressed an interest in getting into the trade and wanted a shop, when given the chance, got cold feet. We reaped the benefit of his indecision.

There was considerable pressure to act quickly to get this lease signed, as the competition from other dealers to take up the lease was intense. We did not have the luxury of negotiation, nor the time to engage a solicitor to act for us. So, I went ahead and signed the lease with a very aloof solicitor who, to be fair, did advise me that I should have legal representation.

I was afraid that any delay would cause us to lose this golden opportunity. Demand for shops from the antique trade on New Hall Lane at that time was such that we felt if we lost this one, we might not get another opportunity. And this was the most impressive shop on the lane, with good frontage and large shop windows.

I signed the lease for three years at a rent of £500 per calendar month, and was responsible for all repairs. This could have been cause for great concern, and I should at least have had an independent professional check on the condition of what I was taking on. But as I have said, time was of the essence. This was 1979, and so we were to have the shop until 1982. We were about to enter the most important and frantic three years of our journey.

We got the keys a couple of weeks later, and during this time we were frantically finishing and polishing stock. We also had another delivery to do to Stamford, which by now was expanding significantly.

The shop itself needed a lick of paint. It had originally been two properties that had been knocked through, with two large downstairs rooms, an upstairs showroom, another room upstairs which made a good tearoom / office, and a small room at the back which we used as a polishing room. I enlisted the help of another young dealer, who had a very small shop on the lane and who was eager to earn some extra cash, to help me get the painting done.

When we entered the property, we discovered the cellar which, to our horror, was full of mould from floor to ceiling. This, as I was to discover, was Rot. Wet Rot - Dry Rot - the lot!

When I spoke to the owner, Mr Cazoogie, he looked at me in amazement. 'Cellar? What Cellar?' He had owned the property for several years but had never been aware that there was a cellar - let alone the fungus in it.

My young helper and myself, shovels at the ready, tackled the fungus, removed it, and sprayed the whole basement. Then we set about painting the outside and organising the sign writing on the widows. Mr Cazoogie was well impressed.

All this was in addition to sourcing and preparing the furniture, not only to stock the shop but also to send to Handsome Pine.

We Did It.

Including the finished items which we had bought from Primrose Antiques, we managed to open our shop with a very impressive display.

When I next spoke to Tony from Handsome Pine, I told him about taking on the new shop. He was a little concerned as to whether we would still want to supply him, but I was able to assure him that he was our number one priority. Tony's father lived in Longton, which is close to Preston, and Tony still came up to see him regularly and would visit the shop on these occasions.

Wyn was still working for us in Fox Street, and she would polish furniture in the back room while she was there. She was never idle - a godsend really. But she had made it clear that she did not want to go to New Hall Lane; she did not drive and thought it would be too difficult to travel there. She had enjoyed her time at Fox Street, but she had only come as an interest - and was ready now to call it a day.

So it was that after a period of probably eight or nine months of running both shops, we gave notice on Fox Street. The Christian Book Centre, which was adjoining, took over the whole premises, and we concentrated our efforts on New Hall Lane.

It was in November of that first year at New Hall Lane that one day, when setting off for Primrose Antiques with a load of pine on the trailer, a car came out of a side street on Fishwick Parade and hit the front of the Granada so hard that I found myself up against the tree in somebody's front garden looking at the sky.

The other driver turned out to be a footballer from Preston North End. His passenger was obviously hurt and needed hospital treatment following the collision. I rang the police and Cathy from the home of the lady whose garden my car had violated.

Cathy ran across the road from our shop to Terry's shop. He immediately came and collected the trailer loaded with furniture. He parked it up at the side of our shop, and later that evening took it back to the barn for me. My car was completely undriveable, so when the police were done and the ambulance was gone, I was left standing with the car until Leyland garage could come and tow it away, which took them about two hours.

Whilst waiting for the recovery, another dealer, Neil Duckworth, came driving by. We did not know each other very well, but when he saw me standing there he reversed back and enquired if I was ok. He then stayed with me until the garage finally arrived. This small act of kindness, together with Terry dropping everything he was doing to move the trailer from the scene, shows again the kindness shown to us by most dealers in the antique trade. They were, and still are, a grand bunch.

The accident presented us with a problem as, for the time being, we had no transport. I arranged to hire a vehicle from Avesco, the company that I used for my one-day van hirings for deliveries to Handsome Pine. However, I decided to seek the advice from my insurance broker friend, Alan Prescott Casson, who I had first met when he worked for Royal Sun Alliance and who had helped enormously when I was seeking cover for the Fox Street shop.

His advice proved to be vital. He felt that, as the other party was a professional footballer, although clearly at fault he would probably escape prosecution. I should engage a solicitor without delay. Certainly, at the time of the accident the other driver had been very arrogant.

Alan gave me the name of a solicitor who he knew to be an expert in this sort of incident, Ian Yates of Ingham Clegg and Crowther, was based in Winckley Square Preston. A telephone call to Mr Yates proved very fruitful. Shortly after introducing myself and telling him a bit about myself and the incident, he realised that he knew our shop. His wife had bought several items of furniture from us, and he would be happy to represent us.

On hearing the details, he promised that he would not charge me if he was not successful. This was, in effect, no win, no fee - unheard of in those days, and his assistance was to prove vital. He advised me to only hire a vehicle similar to the insured, otherwise I would be unlikely to reclaim the cost. I was to pay each week for the vehicle, and he would then claim it back along with any other expenses and an amount for loss of earnings, which he would put at £400. After several twists and turns during which the other side claimed that my car had been driveable (which it clearly was not), a threat to sue finally saw them pay up.

I was without my car for seven weeks, partly because of difficulty in obtaining parts, and also because the Christmas holidays caused a delay. The series of delays and the difficulties that they caused at such a busy time, and not being able to use my trailer, nudged me into thinking about getting a van for myself.

A chat with Avesco brought about the decision to lease a Luton van for three years from them. The fee included signwriting, which they would do for me. Instead of hiring several times a month, I would have a van with my name on it for everyday use. It certainly raised a few eyebrows on the lane when I first arrived at the shop with it.

There was already considerable amazement from the other dealers on the lane at the sheer quantity of pine going in and out of our shop. Just opposite our shop, the whole row of properties was occupied at that time by antique dealers, who watched with interest all the comings and goings that were happening at ours. Tony was taking one or two loads every month, and additionally we had attracted many overseas buyers, which was of course one of the main objectives in taking the shop on New Hall Lane.

Over subsequent months, I would often return from my weekly trip to Primrose Antiques and pull up outside of what was, effectively, an empty shop - with virtually every piece of stock sold and gone! And Cathy sitting there waiting for me with a bag full of cash.

Dutch dealers in particular were strong buyers of stripped pine, and it was not unusual for them to buy practically everything in the shop. Cathy would panic a bit because the shop was empty, but we would quickly unload a few bits of the finished stock which I was, by now, regularly buying from Primrose Antiques - and the shop started to look like a shop again.

Private customers who happened to be in the shop when the overseas buyers were at work were staggered at what they saw. As we were too. We could not have dreamed of such a turnover.

This wave of ever-increasing sales did mean a lot of work. Every piece we processed had to be sourced, carried, stripped, collected, carried again, dried, sanded, repaired, polished, and then carried again into the shop.

We had to arrange help with collecting the children from school, and we were fortunate indeed that parents of the children's friends would look after them after school for an hour or so. In particular: Henry and Dorothy Deacon, Pauline Close, and Mrs Hunter and her daughter Jane - who later looked after the children every Saturday. We were grateful for such help.

Our sons, David and Kevin, and several of their friends, were very good at the sanding and polishing. It was very cost-effective, but the boys could make good money. I seem to remember I paid them about £5 for each item, so they were each able to earn £20 to £30 on a Saturday. Between us all, we processed an astonishing quantity of finished goods from Victorian pine boxes, to pine wardrobes, and everything in between.

The quantity that Tony sold from Stamford was amazing. My trips there became more frequent, and on several occasions before leasing the Transit Luton I had to hire a huge van which took some filling! We would deliver, get paid, come back, and think we could take it easy for a couple of days. And then Tony would ring up saying he had sold most of it, and when could we come down again?

We gradually managed to fill the large ballroom in the hotel in Stamford, but once this was achieved Tony wanted to keep it full, thus offering plenty of choice. He used the large old dining room as backup storage, so that he could quickly replenish the ballroom as things sold.

He told me once that there were quite a lot of people from London who visited his shop. Stamford was such a historic town so there were always plenty of tourists. This was the time when pine furniture of the antique variety was "The Fashion".

We could never have imagined when Tony bought those first four chests just how significant that sale would turn out to be. Neither, I think, did he ever imagine quite such a money spinner.

I always kept my prices reasonable, covering all the costs but leaving me a margin, and I know from several dealers that I met later that my prices were keen. I never begrudged what profit any dealer buying from me made, so long as they didn't try to beat me down, and paid promptly. Tony never queried the prices, and paid immediately. He was very fair, but he knew he was onto a good thing.

The effect of such an output of sales did however require an increasing supply of old pine furniture 'in the paint.'

There were many other large pine concerns like Primrose Antiques: Addingham Pine, Utopia (who later became one of our customers), Jerry Cox from Colne, among many others. Few had a retailing dealer like Handsome Pine - we were indeed very fortunate. Our presence on "The Lane" gave us access to many other dealers (and knockers) willing to sell pine to us.

One evening we had a knock on the door at our home in Edinburgh Close. There stood our old friend Billy, his car and roof rack fully loaded with Victorian painted pine furniture - exactly what we needed. 'Got some pine, where do you want me to unload it?' was his greeting.

We would need to take it down to the barn, but I explained to Billy that I might not have enough cash on hand to pay him there and then for such a large quantity. 'Doesn't matter, pay me whenever' was his reply. Our reputation and trustworthiness were established... we had achieved recognition, and acceptance in the dealing community.

Another dealer was Jack Blackburn, who had a small shop opposite ours, next to Terry's. Like many others in the trade, Jack had a few strange and cheap-to-rent storage places.

Jack's storage was a couple of old hen cabins... literally in the middle of a field at Kirkham. Having previously brought a few pieces to our shop door to sell to us, Jack was the next dealer to offer me a large amount of furniture. I was invited to go and meet him at the hen cabins, which, as I said, were literally in the middle of a grass field. Once again, I was able to buy a large quantity of good pieces of painted Victorian pine. Just what the market required. I went there on several occasions, each time buying some quality pieces of furniture.

We were at the epicentre of a very busy trade, and it did not go unnoticed that we were moving large quantities of furniture fast, and so an increasing number of dealers started calling at the shop, both to buy and to sell to us. One such dealer was Brian Wolfenden trading as Regent Antiques, and coming as he did from about ten miles outside Skipton, he knew Dave Bovingdon at Primrose Antiques very well.

Brian mainly dealt in pine furniture "in the paint" and he travelled all over the North West buying such items and, as I later discovered, sold mainly to Dave at Primrose. It did not go unnoticed by Brian that we were getting the majority of the pine in our area, so when he called into our shop, if there happened to be any furniture stood on the pavement outside where dealers had dropped it off, he was very persistent in trying to buy it and would not take no for an answer.

Any doubts I had about the future of the business were not that the fashion might change, but that the supply of good pine furniture would dry up; after all they weren't making it now and it was all mostly over 100 years old, and mainly coming to the market through the clearances of terraced streets which had been taking place in all the mill towns of the North.

The supply has created a demand, but what if the demand exceeds the supply? So, I decided that I would reserve several of the best chest of drawers from each consignment I bought, and keep them in case of a future supply famine. We built up a huge wall of chests of drawers at the back of the barn, and processed everything else.

However, Brian's persistence paid off when he eventually wore me down, and I sold the lot to him for cash - something I always regretted. All he did was take them and sell them to Dave at Primrose Antiques, which I could have done myself. On the plus side, I did get paid straight away and soon bought more, but I never did manage to build up such a collection again. This transaction did illustrate that there was a trade to be had in just "buying and selling in the paint", and this could help cash flow at times.

John Corrie was another caller. He usually came at the weekends because his main business was transport, but he was a bit of an "entrepreneur" and dabbled in a few different things. Several years later, I found out that he also sold mainly to Dave at Primrose Antiques. There were many other dealers, such as Jerry Cox from Colne who I met around this time and with whom I later did much business. We were also still buying from Derek and Madge, the dealers we had met and become friends with at the very beginning of our venture at Leyland.

One of our dealer friends had a son who had recently left school but had been struggling to find a job. We were asked if we could help. Given that Wyn from the Fox Lane shop had recently left us, we decided to say yes and offer the son a job. It seemed like a good idea. Let's call him Nick - although that isn't his real name for reasons that will become clear. Cathy had already attended a training session with the Inland Revenue so that she would be aware of all the regulations and how to apply PAYE etc.

Nick did not drive, so each morning I would drive about an hour in terms of the round trip to collect him from home, and then the same again every evening. Nick was able to deal with the customers at the shop and he was very good at it. He was also able to undertake polishing in the little room upstairs. This was a big help to us, as by now Cathy was expecting our fifth child, Alison.

The relationship with our neighbours at Edinburgh Close had considerably deteriorated by this time. There had been complaints made to the council about keeping a van on the drive, in addition to claiming that we were working from home, which was not true as we had the shop and the barn for storage and working. These complaints were dealt with in part by our solicitor Ian Yates, who had acted for us after the accident, and partly by letting the ringleader, our next-door neighbour, know that we would fight the matter in the courts. I don't think she relished going public; she was much happier making anonymous phone calls.

By now, I began to realise that we were on the crest of a wave in the business.

We had several regular trade customers: Tony from Handsome Pine, Ben Stothert from Utrecht, and of course our other regular Dutch buyers. Also, a couple of strong French buyers including Philip Gribinski from Paris, who would buy large quantities of stripped pine chests. In addition to these, there was an increasing interest in antique pine from the American market. I knew that it was very unlikely that we would always be in such a strong financial position, so we began to formulate a plan to try and move to a house with more space and no very close neighbours, while we could.

We began to explore the market to see what could be bought on our budget, which our accountant had outlined to be around £32,000. We put our house on the market with Clayton and Booth estate agents from Fox Street, for whom we had done several valuations of house contents for probate and divorce proceedings.

This was another little earner - another string to our bow, which had developed from when we opened our very first shop. Mostly these valuations were uncomplicated and our reports were gratefully received by the estate agents, who had no knowledge of the price of antiques.

The most notable valuation, for probate, was the contents of a bungalow in Marsh Lane at Longton. The owners of this property were business partners, and over several years they had built up a large collection of artifacts, including horse-drawn carriages, carts, traps, and multiple items of taxidermy - many of which were most unusual, including a huge grizzly bear! One of the partners had died, and his family was disputing the distribution of the assets. Clayton and Booth, through me, were representing one of the partners, and Entwistles were representing the other.

The valuations were to be agreed on site by the representatives of both parties. I felt somewhat out of my depth. The other valuer looked very confident and experienced, and was accompanied by his secretary.

I need not have worried! He clearly had no greater certainty as to the value of such unusual items as I did. We formulated a plan, and labelled each item as we went round the property. One of us would suggest a value, and the other would either agree or disagree until we reached a mutually agreed figure.

It worked well! It was a full day's work to catalogue everything inside and outside this amazing property. It was an extremely interesting and rewarding day, and a great pleasure to have the opportunity to see and handle all these extremely rare items and curios.

When I reported back to Clayton and Booth, they were very pleased, having received a really good report from the other valuer, and they instructed me to greatly increase my normal fee when I presented my bill. It was recognised by all sides that this was a unique undertaking.

Back to the sale of our house. When the "For Sale" notice went up, our delightful next-door neighbour danced a jig in the street and chanted 'They're going!' Crazy woman!!

I am sure that she was as frustrated as we were when no viewings were forthcoming for some time.

In the meantime, Cathy's pregnancy was not going well; from about five months she was experiencing high blood pressure, and it was decided that she must stay in hospital every week from Monday to Friday, and was only allowed to come home at weekends. It was during this time that we started house hunting. We had looked at a property in Moss Lane Leyland - a very large house, and another at Clayton-le-Woods, but both needed considerable work, and then another at Euxton, which also needed considerable restoration.

We only had one viewing of our house in Edinburgh Close over a period of about nine months. We continued to be very busy, and I had to see to the children, fitting this in around work. The children were a bit older now, and with the help of Jane Hunter I managed to keep working.

To facilitate the stripping of the furniture we started to go to Enloc Antiques at Colne, where an ex-employee of Primrose Antiques had set up a stripping operation. He was eager to get my business, and so he offered to open in the evenings. Jane looked after the children while

I was able to do the return journey in only a couple of hours, as Colne was nearer than Skipton.

I found out in later years that Dave Bovingdon was very upset about losing my business. I had not realised that I was actually important to him. Most of his business was export and like many other dealers at that time, Dave was experiencing delays in payment from overseas, whereas I was giving him immediate payment of at least £1,000 every week. Dave later went on to found Coach House, an extremely successful business, importing and wholesaling decorative furniture and artefacts from all over the world.

Cathy was still being monitored in hospital and we had no further viewings on the house. We took advice and reduced the price by £2,000, even though we were concerned that this reduction might compromise our choice of properties to buy. But we were desperate to move.

We then had another viewing - only the second viewing in months of the house being on the market. It was an older couple, and they were resident caretakers at Houghton Towers where they paid a "peppercorn rent". They had spent most of their life before that travelling the world, the gentleman having been a naval officer. They were now retiring from this caretaking position, which they had held since he had left the Navy. They had no property to sell but had limited funds and were considered too old to get a mortgage. The upshot was: they could pay £19,000 but no more. This represented a further reduction of £2,000 on our asking price, but they were keen to buy and we were desperate to sell. We accepted the offer. I even took some antique copper ship lights from him to raise some more cash! These I quickly sold for a good profit.

With a great sense of relief, we instructed our solicitors Ingham Clegg & Crowther. The sale was underway - at last!

Chapter 14
The Move. A New Era Begins.

We now had a dilemma – we had sold our house but had not been able to find a new one.

Cathy was still confined to hospital all week, so we had very little time to go house hunting. I scoured estate agents' advertisements and on the weekends, when Cathy was home, we "drove by" those we had short listed. Most of these were eliminated for one reason or another. Mainly because of the proximity of neighbours, but also because we required a minimum of four bedrooms.

A further search through the property pages of the Lancashire Evening Post revealed a thought-provoking advertisement by Oyston's Estate Agents. They had two properties advertised at Longton and although neither had four bedrooms, they both had outdoor space. This promoted the idea, which we had not previously considered, that the outside space offered us the opportunity to extend the property in the future.

A "drive by" at the weekend quickly eliminated one of the properties, which was in Marsh Lane. It was semi-detached and in close proximity to other neighbours, with the land being a very narrow plot to the rear of the property.

In later years of dealing, I was to do business with the couple who did purchase this house, as by coincidence they dealt in antique pine furniture also. It transpired that, throughout all the years of living there, they had long-running battles with their neighbour. More than twenty years and many court battles. We had clearly made the right decision to eliminate this house.

The second property of interest was at Gill Lane, and although we drove up and down the road, we could not find it. The following day, a telephone call to the agents revealed that the owner did not want a "For Sale" sign to be erected. They gave me directions, so when I left the shop that evening I drove past the property, which looked promising - so much so that I arranged an urgent viewing.

I was informed that there was already some interest in this property, so rather than wait until the following weekend when Cathy was home again, I decided to view it myself, together with young David, our 13-year-old.

The viewing went well. A lot to take in.

We had never bought an old property before, but it was generally in good order. It had lots of bright yellow and purple painted surfaces, heavy black and gold flock wallpaper, and net curtains at all the windows which made the house seem dark. But there was nothing that we could not improve.

The main advantage was that it had several large sheds, outside space of one and a half acres, plus an orchard of more than thirty established fruit trees forming a natural barrier between us and the nearest neighbour. But only three bedrooms!

This property ticked lots of boxes but raised other questions. It was on the market for £45,000 which was £13,000 above our price range. There was also the small matter that Cathy had not seen it. During the viewing, the owner had also mentioned several times about that pesky other interested party, who were apparently sufficiently committed to have submitted a planning application for a large extension. This put some pressure on the situation, especially as the sale of our house was proceeding rapidly - our buyers had no mortgage application to process and no house to sell.

I spent the next day at the shop chewing it over and over in my mind. I was under pressure and unable to discuss it with Cathy. I had a major decision to make. Most properties on the market would not fit the bill, and I had this overriding feeling that we should move up the property ladder while business was good - it might not always be so!!

Having agonised all morning, I came to a decision just after lunch; the agents had called me in the morning to see how the viewing had gone, and I had promised to ring them back. I decided to make an offer which would make the decision for me. If they did not accept my offer, then that would be an end to the matter.

I made the call and offered £43,000 - which was £2,000 below the asking price. The agent did that classic deep intake of breath and asked, 'Oh... is that the most you will go to?' I made it absolutely clear that that was it - no more, or I would walk away.

The agent called back before I even had time to make a cup of tea to relieve the stress; my offer had been accepted because I was in a position to proceed immediately.

I had bought a house... and now I just had to break the news to my very pregnant, just about to give birth, wife.

I had made a life changing and very quick decision, but I just had the right feeling about it. My next visit to Cathy involved quite an interrogation... 'What do you mean you've bought a house?'

Trying to describe the house was harder than you can imagine. I had, after all, spent less than an hour there, and could not remember some of the finer details... such as,

'Where is the front door?'
'There is no front door' (there was, I just couldn't remember because we went in the back)
'Are the windows big, or small?'

'Very small.' In fact, the windows were huge. The whole front of the house was virtually glass, but the net curtains had deceived me!!!!

Young David, at 13 years old, had to draw a plan of the house so Cathy had some understanding of the layout. No glossy brochures in those days. I just had the confidence that it was right for us, and in the long term that turned out to be the case.

The main hurdle now was to obtain a mortgage sufficient to complete the purchase, but the amount needed was considerably more than the amount that the accountant had estimated I could reasonably expect to borrow on our earnings.

I made an appointment to see the manager at the Halifax Building Society in Leyland, alone, as Cathy was still hospitalised. Mortgages for self-employed people were difficult to obtain, but the final decision was made at the discretion of the manager. So, I was very anxious at this critical time; we needed to get away from Edinburgh Close, and we had seen no other suitable property any cheaper.

The manager, an attractive redhead, was new. This could be a disadvantage if she turned out to be over cautious. I took my latest set of accounts with me, rather than a tax return. The gross sales and profits were quite impressive, but the net figure after all deductions were much less so. However, my luck was in that day, and after only a few minutes of examining the figures, she announced that there was no problem at all, and she would be happy to advance the full required amount. I shall always believe that she was working on the gross profit - rather than the net earnings figure. It was obviously "Meant to Be".

I had no concerns myself because business at this time was exceedingly good, but my accountant believed that I had pulled off something of a coup! I took the good news to Cathy, and a few days later our second daughter, and fifth child, Alison was born. Having already got three boys, we were all delighted to have a sister for Bernadette, who by now was eleven and desperate for a sister.

Our business continued at a steady pace, and our house sale and the purchase of the new one proceeded without any hold up.

It is worth recording that during these busy times, I still did milk round holiday relief for Norman Yates (quite a lot), Ken Smith and his sister, and Joe Brakewell and his brother. These rounds were all very easy, with reliable lads to do most of the running, so I was able to honour my agreement to provide them with holiday cover - even though at this time I did not need to do it for financial reasons.

Our new home required some improvements which we hoped to be able to do prior to moving in. There was no central heating, and only one socket in the whole house. With a family of young children, it was imperative that we remedy this situation. With the vendor Bill Carr's agreement, I went to the house with an electrician - David Nelson, who we had got to know quite well as his wife had bought several items of furniture from our shop, and we made frequent deliveries to their home.

When we arrived, we were directed to the middle bedroom upstairs where the meters were situated in a high cupboard. David looked at the mass of electrical boxes and meters with only a little less amazement than me. I was deeply alarmed by what I saw, but David reassured me that he could replace it all with a modern consumer unit, his view being that we ought to have it done before we moved in, as it was likely that there would be some disruption over several days.

Bill and his wife had already moved into their new home and there was very little furniture in the property, however Bill was reluctant to agree to this access without first discussing it with his wife. Fortunately, after a few days, he rang me to say that she had agreed.

David, the electrician, was able to arrange directly with Bill the days and times that he could work at the house. He subsequently installed a new ring main and a fuse box, at a total cost of £230. This was all completed a week before we moved in.

The move took place on May 27th, 1981.

Alison was just six weeks old. We were fortunate indeed to have Jane Hunter to help look after her - Jane was later to become her Godmother. While Jane performed childcare duties, Jane's mother helped us to clean the house we were leaving. Young David, Kevin, and David's friend John Hunter helped us with the move, which we conducted ourselves as we had our own van.

Norman Yates, whose milk round I covered most often, helped me to move a few outdoor items the day before, and on the day of the move he helped me to lay bedroom carpets which we had transferred from Edinburgh Close. Norman was more than willing to help with the move, as he had booked me to do a week's holiday relief starting that weekend. All in all, the move went very satisfactorily.

We had done it!!!!!

Our third move since we married, and each house purchase had been a very quick decision. Somehow, I always seemed to know when it was right. My dad often talked about a sixth sense. Maybe there is something in that, I don't know for sure - but certainly in the long run our decisions seemed to be fruitful.

Once we were settled into Hill View our life became even busier. This was an old property, a different experience for us, and there was plenty to do to make it more comfortable. During the first few months we undertook a considerable amount of work to improve the property, including stripping some of the internal doors and basic decorating. We removed a wood burning stove which was situated in the corner of the downstairs reception room, part of which had originally been the larder when the house was built.

The removal of this stove meant that we could make better use of this space as our dining area, and we turned the original dining room into a bedroom for our boys Kevin and Stephen - thus easily converting the house into a four bedroomed property.

Our friend John Beesley was proving very helpful, not only with jobs on the house but also repairing furniture for our business using one of our sheds. We had installed the old corner stove from the house in this shed, so John had a real cosy workshop there, with a ready supply of fuel - wood salvaged from the offcuts of timber.

With John's considerable abilities, we replaced all the downstairs floors (which had been wood laid over and nailed to a coke breeze) with asphalt and concrete, and put in a new damp course. John also replaced all the skirting boards. At this time the only form of heating in the house was the open coal fire in the sitting room, and our next big job was to be the installation of central heating.

Soon, however, there were to be some dramatic setbacks during these first months at Hill View; changes to our fortunes in the antiques business - changes which were to characterize our business as being feast or famine. Further improvements to the house were severely hampered by these changing fortunes.

Sales in the shop had continued steadily, but there was an unexpected shock from Handsome Pine. We had made a large delivery to the ballroom at Stamford shortly after moving into our new house, but then there was a lull, and we did not receive the normal repeat order in the usual way.

When we moved house, our customer from Utrecht, Ben Stothert, had seized the opportunity to instruct us to pack his shipping containers in our yard, rather than have all the furniture he purchased from us transported elsewhere for packing. This made good sense, and we hoped also that it would increase the amount of money that he would spend with us, rather than purchasing from other dealers.

His method of operation was to order in advance: tables, chests of drawers, bedding boxes etc. He would then advise us of the date he would arrive, and on arrival he would produce from his jean's pockets huge amounts of cash.

He travelled light - no luggage, no bags, just his travel ticket and the cash, and when we had packed the container, he would disappear off again on the ferry back to Europe. He had been dealing with us for about 18 months, although prior to our move to Hill View he had packed his containers elsewhere.

At the end of each visit, he was usually one or two hundred pounds short of the full amount, as there were always extra items that he saw when he was looking through our stock. We were happy to allow this credit, as on his return he would immediately pay anything he owed. However, with the last container we packed for him at Hill View, the shortfall was considerably more than this, as it was a 30 ft. container which took a lot more furniture to fill than his normal 20 ft. ones. He promised to pay the balance on his return which would be, usually, in a few weeks. But this time it was to be different. He did not return.

When we spoke on the phone it was obvious that he was in some financial difficulty; sales had slowed for him, but he was optimistic that they would recover soon. However, this never happened, and we never did get paid in full. He did send us £50 on three occasions, but that was it. We know that this decent young man had not set out to cheat us in any way, but that was little comfort when we needed the money.

Worse was still to come.

We had a visit at our home from Tony (Handsome Pine) who wanted to let me know in person that he had managed to sell the pine business in Stamford. A necessity, since their property business was in severe financial difficulty due to the sudden and rapid rise in interest rates that had occurred. Tony assured me that the new owner would carry on buying from us.

Tony and his new family took off for the continent to avoid creditors. It sounds bad, but Tony, even now when he was in trouble himself, always paid me; even that last delivery when, if he had intended, he could have bounced my cheque, but he did not. He made sure that we had every penny due to us. Once again, we had the privilege of dealing with an honourable and decent man. I felt deeply sorry for his situation, but as later events will show our paths did cross again.

The purchaser of Handsome Pine Antiques in Stamford turned out to be a complete waste of time. The first load that I took down he did not pay for, promising to send a cheque, which eventually (after some chasing on my part) I did get, but only several weeks after the delivery. When I enquired of him about buying more, he said 'Yes, and some of what I bought last time I will return as it has not sold'. Needless to say, I did not bother, and did not communicate with him again, nor him with me.

And so it was that only a couple of months after we had moved house, we had lost two of our most important customers through no fault of our own.

It certainly appeared as though our efforts to secure a larger property with some urgency had been the right thing to do. As our financial situation deteriorated, with sales floundering, we would not have been able to secure such a property as we had. It meant that we had a more spacious environment in which to live, and a better investment for the future.

The shop continued to produce sales, but less of the repeat, large volume bulk business which had put us where we were. There was a steady stream of overseas buyers in the area, but not all of them bought pine. When travelling up New Hall Lane to start the day's business, we were often late for our official opening time of 10am. Alison was still only weeks old, and by the time we had got the older children to school, and the baby changed and ready, we were often ten or fifteen minutes late. It was an interesting observation that we would see foreign buyers' vans driving out of the Lane, meaning that we had missed their business, but we mused that by the time we got to the door of our shop, there would be another buyer waiting for us to open, and so there was! In those days, we would never have to worry about missing a buyer - there would always be another, just a few moments later.

When our shop assistant 'Nick' had commenced employment with us, we had ascertained the appropriate and legal statutory wage, and then paid him slightly more than this. Nick had by now passed his driving test and, as I no longer had to transport him each way to and from his home, we increased his wage by a further five pounds a week, and then increased it again when he reached his next birthday. His transport was a small estate car, so he also offered to do customer deliveries on the way home, for which we allowed him to charge the customer five pounds for himself.

Nick was a dab hand at polishing and keeping the shop tidy, so as a treat, while Cathy stayed at the shop, I frequently took him out with me for the day on my buying trips. On these occasions I would always buy him his lunch. I felt he was worth it.

Also, since obtaining his own car, he would bring me any items of pine furniture that his dad (who, if you remember, was a dealer) had procured for me. I was pretty sure that he was adding a bit to the prices, as I knew what his dad's normal rates were, but I did not question this.

As Alison was so tiny, there were occasions when Cathy stayed at home, and while I was out buying, I left Nick in charge of the shop. On my return, I often noticed that there were items where the price label had been removed. Nick's explanation was that he had been repolishing the item, and had removed the label to avoid getting wax polish on it.

His time with us had been mostly pleasant and rewarding for us all, but as time went on, he made ever more increasing demands for higher wages, sometimes aggressively, even though we were paying him over and above the statutory level - not to mention other perks which we were happy to give.

Financially, things were a little tight as we had a bigger mortgage to pay, with increasing interest rates, and we had less regular bulk sales such as those we had achieved with Tony and Ben - customers we sorely missed.

On the plus side, at that time there was an increasing interest for antique pine from American buyers. They did not have the regularity that we had been used to, but shop sales were good. Victorian stripped pine furniture was in huge demand in those days.

Saturdays were especially busy, and we needed more than one or two staff in the shop to deal with customers – it was not unusual to arrive at the shop to find a queue of people waiting to get in. It was occasionally necessary to ask Nick to work on a Saturday, and on those occasions, we paid him cash.

It was a great shock therefore when, one Monday morning, I arrived at the shop to be greeted by a very angry Nick. Cathy and I had spent the weekend looking at things that needed doing at the house and we were lacking the funds to do it, so his outburst was ill-timed. He announced to me that he and his dad had decided that I did not pay him enough, and that if I didn't do something about it, they would!!

I was both shocked and angry at this outburst. We had treated 'Nick' like one of our own, and we ourselves at that time were facing a decline in regular bulk trade sales - on which we had always depended.

My immediate response was yes - I *would* do something about it. I gave him two weeks' notice - two weeks, not the obligatory one week. I do not like anyone putting a gun to my head in that way. A diplomatic approach would have served him better, and at this time we did not need the aggravation.

A week or so after his departure, Cathy was alone at the shop (except for baby Alison) when she received an unwelcome visit in the form of a wages inspector demanding to see the books. This was clearly the enactment of Nick's threat. This development was deeply upsetting for Cathy, even though she knew we had done everything for Nick correctly, and had even gone beyond what was required. She did not deserve to be hurt and upset in this way, and I was having none of it. Battle stations were required.

The inspector made an appointment to call at the shop at 11am the following day, and had left instructions for access to all our records. When he arrived, I was waiting and ready to do battle. We took him upstairs to our office and left him with all our paperwork, having first made it clear that I would not be paying Nick any more money.

The inspector replied, 'You will have to, if I discover that you have underpaid him'. Filled with confidence that we had not done so, I gave the poor man a broadside that I am sure he never forgot.

'You can put me in prison if you want, but he is not going to get another penny'.

The inspector retorted that I would have to, and I retorted that I would not.

I invited him to carry on with his work, but assured him that there would be no payment. We sent him up a cup of coffee, and left him to it.

About two thirty that afternoon he emerged with the words 'I am pleased to say, you have been compliant with your employee's wages. And you have paid him an average of £5 a week over the minimum'.

'In that case' I replied, 'I want it back!'
'No, no, no' he retorted, 'it doesn't work like that.'
'You told me that I would have to make good any underpayment, so it follows, to me, that he should have to make good any overpayment' - although of course I knew it didn't.

The poor man must have gone home with a big headache that day. But my anger was really towards Nick, and the inspector just happened to be collateral damage. I felt very bitter. I had given Nick a job when he needed it and treated him just like my own sons. To make matters worse, it was not long after this that I discovered the real reasons why the labels were sometimes removed from the stock in the shop.

Most of our customers visited us regularly since our stock was unique and ever changing. We discovered from several of these regular customers that there were discrepancies between the prices that Nick was quoting, and the prices that were on the original label.

He had been asking higher prices than the label prices to the customers, and then telling me that he took an offer less than the label prices - and pocketing the difference. The matter came to light when a regular customer came back in, having purchased something previously from Nick. A remark that she made about the item she had bought made me suspicious. When I next delivered an item that she had bought, I asked her if she had the receipt for any of the items she had purchased from Nick. One of the items was a very unusual piece of furniture, and I immediately spotted that she had paid Nick £40 more than he had told me. I did not let the customer know about this discrepancy.

The most unfortunate result of all this, was that it ruined our relationship with his parents, who we had been friends with - and done much business with - over many years. They stopped dealing with us. I did tackle Nick's dad about it several years later, in an attempt to clear the air. He said I should have brought the matter to him at the time, and in any event, he never spoke to me again.

His son had not only been paid above the statutory wage, but was also paid cash for deliveries, and for working on Saturdays, not to mention all the free lunches. It had helped our friends by providing their son with a job, and in turn he had been a big help to us – it had worked well. What is passed is done, and I would like to remember them in a good light. That's life!

Some time later, I heard from my old friend, Matt, who had kept in touch with Nick's parents, that Nick's mum had died, but I know his dad was still around in 2019. I had seen him at Warren and Wignalls with one of his carers. I wish him well - and always did.

From the start of our time in New Hall Lane, as well as regular buyers, there had been dealers calling to sell to us, such as Bell Antiques from Grimsby selling pine and clocks, and Colin Robinson from nearby Hull.

We progressed to visiting both these dealers at their own premises, to get to the source and secure the best items. On one trip alone to Colin's, we filled our Luton van to the roof with good quality pine - mostly knock-down wardrobes which sold well to our private buyers as well as to Handsome Pine, spending over £5,000 on that one trip. This was a considerable amount of money in the early 1980's.

We also dealt with Phillip and Paul Alison, who owned Preston Antique Centre at that time. Although their business was welcome it was sporadic. The shop was still extremely busy, and we were selling well, but we were missing the regularity of large orders.

Times were definitely changing.

Chapter 15
A Diversification.

When we moved to Hill View in May 1981 with the prospect of many improvements to be carried out, plus repair work for the business, our friend John Beesley decided that he had had enough of climbing ladders and dodging rain, and sold his window cleaning round to concentrate in his other skills in DIY etc.

It was a big blow to us both then, when due to the slowing of business, it became apparent that I wouldn't be able to guarantee work for him. John was adamant that he was not returning to window cleaning, and in the conversations which followed I remarked that the only other thing that I had to fall back on was the milk business, and the relief work which I had undertaken for some of the private dairymen in Leyland.

There were still some essential jobs to be done in the property, and we had commenced replacing the floors and the skirtings in the downstairs rooms. As we worked, the idea was conceived about the possibility of buying a milk round for ourselves.

One of the private dairymen, Ken Smith, had three rounds in Leyland, and had branched out into the footwear business and opened a shop. He had decided to sell one of his rounds to release capital. The asking price was £24,000.

John and I decided to express an interest in the purchase, and Ken brought his paperwork for us to examine. Obviously, this would require a bank loan. It was a shock when, three days later, Ken returned, collected his books, and said that he was unable to sell us the business.

By this time (1981), following a strike at Unigate's main depot, most of these private dairymen had ditched Unigate as their supplier and set up a consortium, backed by the Milk Marketing Board. They set up a shared fridge facility on Leyland Lane, and the consortium (known as The Group) had decided that they would endeavour to control all the milk distribution in Leyland. As such, they decided that John and I would not be allowed to join them.

Instead, they decided to buy Ken's round and split it up between themselves.

I was hurt, and angry, I considered them all to be friends. I had, after all, performed holiday relief for nearly all of them during the previous three years since I had left Unigate.

As Ken left our house, he apologised - to which I retorted: 'By Christmas, we will have a milk round in Leyland.' I didn't really believe that, even myself, but that remark turned out to be very prophetic.

A few days later, John arrived at our house with quite an air of excitement, which was out of character for him. He had, by sheer chance, met a dairyman who was not part of the Leyland consortium, as he was based in Eccleston. This dairyman wanted to sell a small part of his round, comprising fifteen gallons a day, so that he could consolidate his business in Eccleston. The area that he wanted to sell was Midge Hall, in its entirety. This was indeed very exciting for us, as it was right on the doorstep of Hill View - the last part of Leyland before reaching the Longton area. He delivered to every single house in Midge Hall - there was no competition.

The price he was asking was three thousand pounds, which neither we nor John had. However, at this point, we still had our income from the shop, and our credit was good with the bank. John and I were in agreement that this gallonage could be a starting point, and as the Moss Side area of Leyland (which is adjacent to Midge Hall) was being developed under the Central Lancashire Plan, there was huge potential to grow it and expand.

And so it was, with the assistance of a bank loan of £3,000, that R&B Dairymen was born. Although "The Group" did everything they could to prevent it, we managed to secure the purchase of a second-hand industrial fridge, which John and I erected in the yard behind our house, and for which John made a very effective weatherproof covering.

A Local Authority Licence was obtained, despite attempts by Norman Yates (of all people) to frustrate its issue, and a deal was struck with Lancashire Dairies for supply. Lancashire Dairies were based in Manchester, and they were the supplier to Frank - who we had bought the fifteen gallons from. They were keen to expand in our area, so backed us with free milk offers to gain business.

My prophecy to have a milk round in Leyland had come to pass.

By the time we took our first delivery, we were already up to twenty gallons a day. John had secured all his family's business, and our friend Matt also gave us his business.

We did not feel the need to acquire a vehicle for delivery to begin with. I used my estate car, and John used his own vehicle too. It was a "cash" business, so money was coming back into our account from the end of the first week and, to begin with, we took no wages out of it.

With the bank loan and a month's credit from the dairy, we were soon able to consider the purchase of a vehicle. I was still running the shop and polishing pine, so John did lots of research into suitable vehicles, which led us to decide on a little Honda Acty pickup, a small but nippy little open backed van.

We went to the Honda dealer at Southport, which was one of the leads that John had investigated, from where we purchased our first little milk float for the princely sum of £2,800 brand new!

John took on his new role with great enthusiasm and his canvassing skills very quickly became apparent. He and his wife Margaret, and Cathy and I, took it in turns to go round the new housing developments in Moss Side several times a day, so anyone moving in was accosted and offered a couple of weeks free milk. We gained new customers steadily, and by Christmas 1981 we were delivering about 35 gallons per day.

This first winter at Hill View saw a very heavy snowfall, and the road between Midge Hall and our home was closed for a full day. We had taken the precaution of delivering the milk the evening before. We set off at about 5pm, and when we finished around 8pm Midge Hall was cut off completely. Young David and I had to abandon the milk float and trudge home on foot through the deep snow, only to find there was a power cut at the house which added to the feeling of complete isolation.

We also sold eggs - purchased from the egg farm next door to Hill View, potatoes - purchased from one of our customers, Paul's Farm at Cocker Bar, and additionally we began to sell soft drinks, all in an effort to boost profits. To begin with, and for some time, John and I took turns to deliver the milk, doing alternate weeks each.

On the weeks that I was not delivering milk, I would continue working intently with the pine furniture - sourcing, stripping, repairing, and polishing. Although the shop business continued, we had never managed to replace the steady volume of sales which had been achieved with Handsome Pine.

We entered 1982 with steady expansion of the milk round. John had discovered that the social housing, rented out by Central Lancashire Housing Association, issued the keys to new tenants on Tuesdays. John came to an agreement with the canvasser employed by Unigate, so that one of us would cover the mornings and Les (the Unigate canvasser) covered the afternoons. This ensured that someone was outside the Housing Association office all day, and as the tenants exited with the keys, we canvassed for their milk order.

Any orders achieved for Clayton Brook and the surrounding area were passed to the Unigate rep, and most of the Moss Side orders were ours. This worked well, and together with watching any "Sold Houses" in our area (we went out every evening also) we steadily built up our business.

During the early part of 1982 we sent for Maggie, our sixth child, and she was expected to arrive in October.

With 'Nick' now gone, it fell to Cathy to attend the shop every day. To help with cleaning the house in preparation for this latest addition to our family, we answered an advert by a lady who did a "one off" cleaning service. This was Anne, who by coincidence was the wife of another milkman in Leyland who had sold his round to "The Group". Anne suited us well, she was a godsend, and ended up staying with us for over a year, and only left to start her mature training as a nurse. She was sorely missed when she left.

The milk business was, at this stage, only intended to be a side-line, and we continued to run the shop. We continued to get some unexpected sales. Late one afternoon, a large van pulled up outside. A young couple entered the shop and introduced themselves as dealers who had a successful shop in Edinburgh. Their business was mainly retail, and they were eager to source pine which was already stripped and finished.

They had arrived at our shop purely by chance, and were very impressed with the stock that we carried. We had some exciting Scandinavian antique pine, which we had obtained through our dealings with Dave Bovingdon at Primrose Antiques. We also had a range of hand-built pine reproductions made from reclaimed timber from Max, a contact who traded from the town of Rugby. And so - we had an exclusive stock of quality furniture.

It did not take them very long to start buying from us, and they did not leave until well after closing time - by which time they had spent more than £2,700 on this, their first visit. They loaded their van and paid in cash with Scottish banknotes, mainly in denominations of £100 and £200 pounds. The money was very colourful – we had never seen these kinds of banknotes before.

The next morning, I went directly to the bank to pay it in. I was well known at the bank and was on first-name terms with all the staff. I handed the cash over. The bank teller, Mary, examined it then passed it in turn to each of her colleagues to examine. In total, four of the staff examined it for what seemed a long, long time.

I began to panic. I was sure they must be fake. When the banknotes finally returned to Mary, who was dealing with me, I had to ask, 'What's wrong?'

She replied, to my obvious relief, 'Nothing - we just have never seen these notes before.'

The Scottish couple, Ian and Marie, came several times after that, once coming back to Hill View for tea - until they too became victims of the impending recession.

The hand-built pine reproductions to which I referred were sourced from Max, who had been introduced to me by Tony from Handsome Pine. Other than ourselves, Max was the only other supplier to Handsome Pine. Tony had indicated that he was sure we could sell these items in our shop, so I had taken a trip across the country from Stamford to Rugby, a lovely journey I remember.

I purchased a collection including Spanish style refectory tables in various sizes, and astragal glazed corner cupboards. They did indeed prove to be popular – especially the tables. Each time Ian and Marie came, they bought a couple of pieces from this range. Max was years ahead of his time, and all the furniture was manufactured by hand in reclaimed timber, using traditional construction. We still have one of his astragal glazed corner cupboards and a seven-foot refectory table in our home, nearly forty years later.

The milk round was developing quickly, and the lease of the shop was approaching renewal but sales at the shop were slowing. One of our regular buyers from Holland had been calling every couple of months in his jeep and trailer, purchasing mainly Victorian draw-leaf dining tables from us. He sawed off the legs of these lovely old tables (outside the shop on the back of his trailer!) as they sold them for use as coffee tables back in the Netherlands - and handed us back the legs!!! He had noticed that we sold a lot of the continental "knock-down" wardrobes and cupboards, and commented that he could bring some over on his next visit.

When he did turn up with some, they were absolute rubbish - with woodworm, rot, and an expensive price tag. I told him that there was no way I could use them, but he was not happy as he needed the space on his trailer for other purchases. He asked if he could leave them with us until his next trip over. I refused to allow these items into the shop, but agreed to store them in a lean-to in the backyard, where they were at least out of sight, and the structure did afford some shelter from the weather. He assured me that he would collect them on the next trip but he did not come back for them.

By now we had begun to consider not renewing the lease on the shop, and so to fulfil our obligations we began to clear the premises, including the yard.

Further examination of the furniture we had stored for our Dutch buyer confirmed that it was so rotten that it was no use at all. We had no means of contacting him, we had not seen him for well over a year, and we made the decision to remove and dispose of it.

A few days later, literally, he, and his equally vicious looking colleague, appeared at the shop to reclaim his goods. When Cathy explained the circumstances, he demanded the money for them, which was the £700 pounds he had originally asked, and told her in no uncertain terms that he would be back in the morning for his money, and would not take no for an answer.

I went into the shop the next day, and sure enough this very menacing pair turned up and demanded their money. To which I replied, 'You owe me twelve months storage charge - so we are even.' I questioned why he had never contacted me. He offered no explanation for this. Judging by the appearance of the pair and their menacing looks, I suspected that they had been on an "enforced holiday". After much grumbling and threatening, they eventually left. We were quite convinced that they would return at night and put the windows in. But in the end, all was well.

As the renewal date approached, we made the difficult decision not to renew the lease. Principally this was because the state of the rot and structure of the building caused me great concern, as we had a full repairing lease and one of the walls was in danger of collapse. A prospective new tenant refused to take on a full repairing lease because of the obvious rot problems.

I went with him to see Mr Casoogie, and explained that the rot had been there when I took over the property, and I did not feel that I should be held responsible. Mr Casoogie listened intently, and immediately instructed the potential new tenant to arrange all the repairs and that he, Mr Casoogie, would settle the bill.

I felt a tremendous sense of relief at his decision, but he was aware that we had been good tenants, always paying the rent on time, and had kept it in a good state of repair in terms of what we could control. We were very lucky. It was within his rights to invoke the repairing clause which we had signed. He was a very fair man.

We were sad to leave the shop which had been so productive for us, but with changes in the trade, losing those big wholesale buyers because of changing times, and ever-increasing interest rates, we were squeezed.

Given all this, and the fact that we had embarked on the milk round venture from Hill View, we left 134/136 New Hall Lane at the end of 1982.

Chapter 16
Combining Opportunities.

So it was with some sadness that we left the shop on New Hall Lane.

We continued to sell pine from our barns at Hill View to, among others, Hayden Latham, his American contacts, and to Mrs Robin Griffith - whose family own West Lancs Antiques Exports. She had been one of the shippers frequently bringing trade to the area, and their son Brett still operates the business to this day (2020), working now with *his* son at their base at Burscough. In later days, we also dealt extensively and directly with other American customers. At this time, we also continued to concentrate on expanding our milk business with John Beesley.

We were still hampered by a lack of funds to get much of the improvement work done on the house. We did manage to replace one of the tumbledown sheds with another large ex-hen cabin, some sixty feet in length, which we purchased from our neighbours Jean and Tom Leigh. We re-erected this hen cabin on a new concrete base, with help from our neighbours. This gave us some more dry storage, which was much needed.

The milk business, although growing steadily, did not produce a living for both John and ourselves. John supplemented his income with various DIY jobs, including some for us on the house, when we could afford it.

We decided (as well as continuing to deal in the pine furniture, and the milk business) to utilise the old greenhouses and the land to grow crops for sale. Cathy proved to be very good at growing plants from seeds, and we sold trays of bedding plants at the gate. We also sold tomatoes and cauliflowers, some of which we purchased from neighbouring wholesale growers, to several of the many small shops in and around the New Hall Lane area. Many of these shops were family businesses, and given a good price and good quality produce, they became regular customers.

When Maggie was born in October 1982, we still had Anne doing the cleaning for us, and with a new baby, and all the other labour-intensive things we were doing at that time, she was a godsend. We were aware that she was waiting for her nurse training to begin, and within a couple of months she was gone.

The plant growing continued into another season, and Cathy was able to get lots of useful advice from one of our milk customers in Jane Lane at Midge Hall, who grew bedding plants commercially in several large greenhouses. We were able to buy stock from her at wholesale prices, and sell it for a profit. We also bought fruit and veg from the wholesale fruit market in Preston, which we also sold on.

When Maggie returned home from the maternity hospital, the visiting midwife, on noticing that we dealt in antiques (from our sign-written van) remarked that her father had died recently and that she and her sister were in the process of clearing his house - would we be interested in having a look?

We bought everything they wanted to dispose of, including a brand-new single bed which young David had the use of for about ten years. Other modern items were passed on to a second-hand dealer in New Hall Lane, who we knew. The antique items were sold on to other contacts, and some very useful pounds were earned.

One of the items I purchased (for £10) was a glazed Victorian bookcase top. I remarked that it would have been £50 if it had had its base. To which the midwife's sister replied that she had a similar item, complete with base, and would that one be worth £50? I replied that it would. The bookcase top I had purchased was only about three feet in width, relatively small, so when I was asked to go to her house in Leyland to view the other bookcase, I expected a very similar thing. The property itself was a smallish semi-detached bungalow, and she had indicated that the bookcase was in the spare bedroom.

So, imagine my surprise when I entered the room to see an enormous two-part pitch-pine bookcase, of Gothic form, possibly ecclesiastical, and in excellent condition. She confirmed that she had bought it some years earlier from a vicarage. It was a glazed-top cupboard on a base, about six to seven feet in length, and about six or seven feet tall. Somewhat bemused, I asked her 'What do you want for it?' Her reply was that I had suggested £50 with the base, and that is what she wanted.

The deal was done. I was more than happy with it, and so was she as she wanted the space.

Fortunately, I had with me that day the second-hand dealer (Jim from New Hall Lane). We were returning from a delivery which I had undertaken for Jim, so between us we managed to get this beast of a thing out of this small property, down the garden path, and into the van. How we managed this I will never know, but I do recall that when it was loaded the van was listing heavily to one side.

When I returned home, I left it on the van, obviously. Then I began to wonder what I was going to do with it. I was aching from top to bottom after moving the beast - and didn't fancy moving it again.

Deliverance came in the form of West Lancs Antiques. Mrs Griffith had asked me if I would strip and polish some pine furniture for them, and they happened to turn up in our yard the very next day - with two strapping lads. Fortunately, her husband Bill was also with them that day. I enquired if they would be interested in buying a pitch-pine bookcase. Without much enthusiasm, he agreed to "have a look". However, when I opened the van, his expression changed. I could see he was impressed. 'How much?' he asked. '£150' I replied.

With no argument at all he produced the cash. The two strapping lads, with much groaning and sweating, transferred the bookcase from one van to the other, and then they, and my very heavy piece of furniture, were gone.

The diversity of income continued. Our neighbours from the poultry farm, Jean and Tom and family, often came down and bought orange juice and the odd pint of milk. They wanted to support us as we were buying an increasing quantity of eggs from them, but did not feel that they could sack their milkman - who they had had for years. This was totally understandable.

On one of their visits, they mentioned that they had a relative in Penwortham whose aunt had died, and they wanted the apartment clearing. Thinking that a flat would not yield much of antique interest, I did not respond straight away. But when they asked again, I decided that I had better go, even though we were extremely busy with all the ventures we had going on.

The visit proved to be another pleasant surprise. There was a considerable amount of genuine antique furniture, including a large Georgian writing bureau. I gave individual prices for all that I wanted to buy, and offered to transport all the modern items to the local auction free of charge, and have the auction proceeds paid directly to them.

They accepted all my offers except for the bureau, which Tom wanted to keep for himself. I transported the bureau to their house, free of charge. The job was done, and I did well out of it.

The only undecided item was a TV which was only four months old. I advised them to try to sell it privately. When they received the proceeds from the auction, they were well pleased, and came down to let me know and thank me. They had not managed to sell the TV, and offered it to me for £25. We jumped at it. We had that TV for many years, and later passed it on to our son Kevin when he got his own house - and he, after several years of use, in turn passed it on to our son Stephen. A good deal all round.

During this time, we were still leasing the van from Avesco. We decided we could no longer continue making the lease payments on the van, which we were now only using occasionally. We had of course by now purchased the Honda Acty milk float, and we also had our estate car.

Avesco gave us the opportunity to purchase the van at a very reasonable price, but I decided that we could not raise the money. So, reluctantly, we decided to end the lease and return it. After four years of use it was still like new, so I guess someone got a bargain.

The milk round continued to grow, and we found it necessary to acquire another milk float and split the round into two. Although this meant that John and I would both be delivering every morning, it would enable us commit to the job completely, in pursuit of taking a reasonable wage out of the business, which by now seemed a real possibility.

John and I had a few mornings of fun researching the motor auctions at Walton Summit. Eventually, after a couple of visits, we decided that the time was right, and we spotted coming up for auction a six-month old Honda Acty pickup with only about three thousand miles on the clock.

Being aware that the price of a new Honda Acty was around three and a half thousand pounds by this time, we got very excited when the bidding started at under one thousand pounds. So I was in! Bidding at auctions was second nature to me, and it took only a few minutes and some brisk head nodding to secure the vehicle. The hammer went down to me at only one thousand six hundred pounds.

However, in our enthusiasm, we made the classic mistake of not reading the conditions!!!! When the auction steward approached us with his hand held out for the immediate cash deposit, we were flabbergasted!!! Oh dear (or words to that effect).

He escorted us to the office, where, with heads hung low, we pleaded ignorance.

It was clear to them that, as far as motor auctions were concerned, we were complete novices. They gave us an hour to return with the cash. We scuttled back to our bank in Leyland, where we raided every penny we could raise out of the accounts. We sheepishly slunk back into the auction room office, where we handed over our cash, and were unceremoniously handed the keys and the logbook of the Acty, along with a glare which spelt out 'Get it right next time lads'.

The pickup, which turned out to be a repossession, was immaculate and it never gave us a moment's trouble. So now we had a milk float each.

Shortly after this, Cathy and I decided to concentrate our efforts on the milk business, as the antiques business was a little uncertain. Furthermore, we were working hard on our house as well as out canvassing for milk customers at every possible moment - mornings, afternoons, and evenings. We decided to take a break from our antique business, which was to last for almost three years.

The milk business became our main income for the next few years. It was a modest but regular income, which helped during this period of high interest rates when our mortgage payments had leapt upwards. It was steady work, but relentless - six early mornings a week delivering the milk, and three full evenings a week collecting the money. Some mornings I started at 2.30am.

Our canvassing became ever more successful, especially when we secured exclusive access to people moving into some brand-new housing developments on Moss Side, Leyland. This enabled us to deliver to every house on these estates, thanks to the assistance of the sales negotiators on Fernleigh, Blaydyke, and Fossdale Moss. This was much to the annoyance of our arch-rivals.

John, in the meantime, had likewise secured the Leyland Gates development, together with another new development off School Lane, Leyland. When we split the round into two separate parts, I had kept the Moss Side and Midge Hall areas, and John retained everything on the Leyland side of the "new road" Schleswig Way.

John later moved from their home on Fox Lane to a house on Paradise Lane Leyland, where he installed a commercial fridge inside his garage. This enabled him to maintain his independence, and of course we remained friends.

The intensity of the milk round was very tiring. Cathy and I, and our son David, were all heavily involved, but at least we had a regular income. We maintained this steady expansion and intense work level for about a further four years.

Somewhere around this time, my thoughts began to turn again to the antiques trade. The value of milk round had grown in line with the increase in customers, and had become a very real financial asset. Selling the goodwill in the milk round was a tempting proposition as John and I had now reached the magic target of one hundred gallons a day... each! A remarkable achievement indeed!

I was having the same "gut feelings" towards cashing in the business that I had when we bought Hill View. I kept thinking that it was the right thing to seriously consider.

The consensus in the industry was that the value of the goodwill equated to a sound pension pot when you reached retirement, and in the meantime the business would maintain a steady income for those seeking self-employment.

Personally, I had doubts.

I had no crystal ball, but more and more people were buying milk at the supermarkets, which undercut the price of milk delivered to the door.

Although there had been a huge commitment in time, the only financial investment for myself and John had been £1,500 each. The free milk incentive to new customers was largely backed by our suppliers. Over time, we had purchased another two milk floats between us, so we now had four in total. This enabled both Cathy and John's wife Margaret to also do the deliveries and collect the money independently.

In between the daily routine we had managed to get an extension put on our house, incorporating a kitchen and a dining room, for a very reasonable £2,500. This was built by a milk customer of ours, a builder who lived at Midge Hall. "Stan the builder" was able to do it for this very reasonable quote if I did the labouring for him. That was fun!!! And a few months of even more extensive physical work. He worked hard and was there every day until it was finished. He did an excellent job - but of course he was assisted by my good self!!!

Alison and Maggie, who were about four and three years old at this time, christened our builder "Stan, Stan, the Working Man". They thought this was hilarious. He was highly amused by their chanting it to him. And that is how he is still known to us to this day. He was indeed always working, sometimes having his tea with us to save him from stopping, even though he only lived just around the corner.

Eventually, the extension was finished. But not without a bit of drama!

The work was done, and on the very last day the electrician was connecting the wiring, when a knock came to our door. It was the "Building Inspector"… a frightening sight. He wanted to know what we were up to at the rear of our property???? We had replaced a glass "lean-to" conservatory as part of the new extension but, apparently, we still should have applied for planning permission.

There were a few nail-biting weeks of anxiety while the building inspector debated several aspects: the ratio of glass windows to the room area and the depth of the foundations were some of the issues.

However, the inspector agreed that all was in order. Plans were hastily drawn up by a colleague of Stan, and retrospective planning permission was granted. All's well that ends well.

Early in 1986, with the Christmas rush behind us, I made the definite decision to test the market and advertise my milk round for sale. John had decided to carry on with his own round. Over the next couple of months, we had a few enquiries - all of which came to nothing. However, around March, we hooked what seemed to be a serious contender. This inquiry came from a dairy farmer, whose farm was being compulsory purchased for building development. Although the farm was rented, he had sold his cattle and milk quota, and as a result he had sufficient funds.

Having made the decision to purchase, he agreed to spend four weeks with me to learn the business and the routes etc. He had been used to early morning starts, but was not the athletic type, and I wondered if he would ever make a milkman. Against all the odds, Tony completed the four weeks with me. He was there every morning, on time, but I could see that the finer points of being a milkman were not in him.

On the last Friday of his learning curve, I managed to prise the cheque from him, and gratefully put £33,000 into our Halifax account. However, even this was not without drama. The cashier, who was a milk customer, knew us well. But she was completely thrown by the amount of money and refused to process the cheque without consultation with the bank manager.

Myself, Stephen, and the two girls Alison and Maggie, celebrated our good fortune by going off for a week's holiday at Porthmadog in our caravan. This was summer 1986.

When Tony had committed to buying the milk round, I had to inform our suppliers, Lancashire Dairies, that he had arranged to buy his milk elsewhere. The area manager at Lancashire Dairies offered me a contract job delivering to several supermarkets and some of the smaller shops which they supplied. This covered an area from Poulton-le-Fylde to Chorley with Leyland and Preston in between. Tony had declined to buy the milk vehicles from us, which meant that we had still got a vehicle for this contract. We sold the older Honda Acty and retained the newer one. The dairy paid one and a half pence per unit delivered, so I had a small income after selling the round while we deliberated our next move.

Cathy took on the task of delivering the first week of this contract, so that I could have a break (that week away with Stephen and the girls in the caravan). As we type this, we are completely bemused about how she managed to do it. The shops and petrol stations we delivered to were in Poulton-le-Fylde, Kirkham, several different parts of Preston and Leyland, and a few in Chorley! A large area to cover, and a round trip of approximately 50 miles. Given Cathy's sense of direction, this is nothing short of a miracle. No mobile phones in those days. No sat navs!!!

By now, if you are still reading, you will have realised that whatever I have achieved I could not have done it without Cathy. She has always been my crucial support.

Chapter 17
The Transition.

We had achieved quite a lot since moving to Hill View, but not without hiccups!

Sadly, just before handing the milk round over, my mum passed away quite suddenly. She had been ill for only a short period of about six weeks. Cathy had gone down to Cambridge by train to help look after her, and to take some of the strain off my dad and be company for him. It was sad that being so busy I had not had the opportunity to go down to see her in recent times but, with the milk round now sold, I intended to remedy that as soon as the hand-over was completed. However, that was not to be, she died just before that could happen.

Once again, Cathy had saved the day by being there when I was unable to be. On the day before the funeral, we delivered a double quantity of milk (we still had the main round at this point - this all happened just before the handover was scheduled) so that I could have the day off to attend.

The complexities of life are such that, on this very day, Bernadette was admitted to hospital as an emergency. I had taken her to our local doctor as Cathy was still in Cambridge with my dad. The doctor called for an ambulance to come to the surgery immediately to take Bernadette to hospital, he feared a clot on her lung, which could move at any time.

On arrival at Royal Preston Hospital, she was transferred straight away to Blackpool. So, there we were, Bernie in hospital with things looking very serious for her, Cathy in Cambridge, and I had to get to my mother's funeral, which was the next day.

Whilst of course we were desperately worried about Bernadette, who was about seventeen at this time, this sudden and totally unexpected illness created another dilemma for us. Our plan had been to leave Bernadette looking after the two girls whilst I went down for the funeral, bringing Cathy back home with me afterwards. The girls, Alison and Maggie, were aged about five and three, and we had absolutely no qualms about leaving them with their big sister. She had always been wonderful with the girls, and was like a second mother to them - a great help to Cathy by looking after them, dressing and feeding them etc.

So, we had to formulate another plan very swiftly.

Cathy came back on the train that afternoon, and I travelled down to Cambridge the following day for mum's funeral. The three boys, David, Kevin, and Stephen came with me. With Mum's funeral over, the following week we handed over the milk round to the purchaser, Tony. We resumed our working lives, but nothing so hard as before. It was now a 6am start instead of 2:30am, and there was no collecting of cash in the evenings. We had a relatively easy time now, because once all the contract shop milk was delivered, I was free all day.

With Stephen's help, during his school summer holidays, we fenced in our large field, and decided to embark on a new adventure. We acquired some sheep.

I answered an advert in the Farmer's Weekly, borrowed our next-door neighbour's trailer, and went to Brinscall to pick them up. Our neighbour, Tom Blackett, was a retired farmer and was renting the house next door to us, Stainfield House, with two fields so that he could continue with a small flock of sheep in his retirement. It was with Tom's help and encouragement that I decided to extend our life's experiences and get involved with some livestock.

When Cathy and I arrived at the farm at Brinscall, it was very much obvious to the farmer that we were amateurs, and new to this shepherding. Although he had never met us before, he offered to loan us a ram to run with the five hill sheep that I had just purchased. I quickly found that these hill sheep were wild, and could jump higher than Zebedee on the "Magic Roundabout". The sheep settled well, and the ram did his job, and then obviously became bored.

A few mornings later when I, acting like a 'proper farmer', went to tend to my flock, I did a head count and very quickly became aware that there were five ewes contently grazing the grass BUT no sign of Boris the Ram anywhere.

I panicked. I had lost the ram so generously loaned by the farmer!!!

Frank Carr, another neighbour - and the owner of Stainfield house, came out of his greenhouse and indicated toward the field at the other side of his property, where Tom Blackett had a flock of over 40 hoggets (young sheep for breeding the following year).

There… in the middle of them all... was Boris!!

What to do??

Tom had gone away for the weekend, but his trailer was in his yard. Frank suggested that I should hitch up the trailer to my car and drive into the field, where we would encourage Boris to get into the trailer. To make matters worse, we were due to take Cathy's dad, who had been staying with us on holiday, to the airport that morning for his return flight home. But I didn't dare leave the ram loose in a field full of innocent young sheep!

Young David, who had been staying with his friend Robert Deacon overnight, fortuitously arrived home with Robert just at that moment, so we had another two pairs of hands. We rushed round, hitched up the trailer, Frank opened the gate, and we drove into the field. An open trailer with four frantic people rushing up and down was not such an attractive alternative to a ram, as a field full of forty young ladies. And he was having none of it!!!!

The clock, meanwhile, was ticking to depart for the airport, but I could not leave the ram there.

We devised a plan that would appeal to his stomach. David hastily ran home to get a bucket of sheep nuts which he placed in the trailer. After about ten minutes of frantic activity in the field, we scattered a few of the nuts on the grass, led a trail, and eventually Boris followed the sheep nuts straight into the trailer. We slammed the gate shut and hastily drove the trailer home to our yard, unhitched it, grabbed Grandad Dornan, and roared off to the airport, leaving David and Robert to keep guard on the errant escapee - by now safely (hopefully) secured in the trailer.

Touching almost 90 miles an hour, we got our visitor safely to the airport and checked in for his flight home.

The very next day I returned the ram to Brinscall, and related our adventure to an amused farmer. He didn't seem at all surprised. He obviously knew a lot more about sheep than we did!

I arrived back home that morning and was told that our neighbour Tom, the owner of the sheep, was back from his weekend away. I had to go round and explain the events that had occurred. Fortunately, Frank had already told him, but Tom did not seem to be bothered. He did not think that any harm had been done to his sheep. He explained that his flock were too young and too immature, and unlikely to be interested in Boris at all. That would probably explain why the ram had decided, in the end, that the food offered in the trailer was the better proposition.

In due course, our five wild sheep all produced a lamb each. One of them would not feed her baby, so Tom advised bottle feeding. Although we could have purchased a milk substitute for the purpose, we decided to use bottled sterilized milk, which we stocked for the milk business. The lamb thrived on it. Maggie and Alison, aged five and six, took no persuading to feed it, and needed no reminding when it was feeding time. They took to it with great enthusiasm.

This lamb, a female, was christened "Lucy the Lamb". She stayed with us for about three years, going on to have twin lambs of her own. She became very crafty and followed the girls everywhere, even into the house. She was also a very naughty little girl. She learned to jump the fence, eat our flowers, and jump back over again. The picture of innocence. It was some time before we discovered that she was the culprit of our disappearing flowers.

During this time, Stephen was at St Joseph's Seminary at Up Holland College as a boarder, and potentially a trainee priest. During the holidays he spent quite a lot of time with me. We were having a much more relaxed time, but we needed more income than that which was provided by our contract to deliver milk to shops. Stephen was keen for me to deal in cars, using the capital released from the sale of the milk round, and on Father's Day that year he bought me a book entitled "Four Wheels to a Fortune". Somehow this idea did not appeal to me. His other idea was buying a house to renovate, and although we looked at a couple, the final decision was never reached. In later years I did regret not following the property route, but you have to make a decision, and go with your gut instinct.

Cathy and I had discussed returning to the antique business, however she was not keen for me to return to stripping antique pine as before, as this involved a huge amount of hard physical work. For about a year, we continued with the combination of contract milk delivering and progressing the jobs to be done around Hill View, whilst at the same time considering our next move.

We purchased an additional larger pickup truck to help with the large volume of bulk milk deliveries to Poulton-le-Fylde, Kirkham etc. Stephen loved this, it had a spacious cab with a bench seat, and to his great delight it even had a radio and tape deck. We used this on several occasions to travel to Grantchester to visit my dad at weekends.

Young David was a great help to us by regularly doing milk deliveries to some of the shops. On one memorable occasion, he managed to write-off our Honda pickup while delivering to Chorley. He skidded on some diesel that must have been spilt from another vehicle, right on a sharp bend on a country road in torrential rain. The Honda spun out of control, and by the 180-degree point it was travelling backwards on the wrong side of the road on the bend. The little Honda crashed (rear-on / head-on) with an immaculate and expensive Porsche coming the other way. The crates of milk landed all over the road - having first rained down onto the roof and bonnet of the said Porshe. When the police attended, they kept falling over on the road - such was the severity of the rouge diesel spillage. Very fortunately, David and the other driver were not hurt, but the damage to the Honda and the Porsche was severe enough for the insurance companies to write them off.

We received more from the insurance company for the Honda than we were expecting. Cathy had loved using the Honda as a run-around. It was, she said, like driving a Tonka Toy - and she missed it. We later bought her an Austin Metro and life returned to normal.

It was fate, and another quick decision, that brought us back to the antique trade. Out of the blue, I received a telephone call from a part-time dealer who had sold us antique pine during our period at the shop. He enquired as to whether we still dealt in antique painted pine, as he had a quantity to sell. Without any hesitation, I immediately replied 'Yes.'

So once again fate played a hand, and the decision to return to the antique business had been made. He lived at Cadley Avenue near Lane Ends in Preston. I went with the pickup and, although a little out of touch with prices, in typical Del-Boy style blagged my way as I went. I bought it all. We then resumed buying at Warren and Wignalls, and swiftly made some very useful new contacts.

It was at this point when fate once again lent a hand. I had a severe disagreement with the representative from Lancashire Dairies, for whom we distributed milk to the shops. We had received many complaints, mainly from the supermarkets, that the plastic bottles used for shop sales were leaking frequently and badly. The lorry driver for Lancashire Dairies who delivered the milk to us for redistribution, assured us that they had had many complaints from other customers. When the rep came to see us, he said it was our fault "as we threw them about". At first, I thought he was joking. When I realised that he was serious I told him to get out, in language that could not be considered ambiguous. I resigned from the contract not long after that, and our transition to returning to full time antique dealing was confirmed.

The irony of the situation was that about a year later, this rep from Lancashire Dairies was convicted of fraud, and given a prison sentence. When he was released, he had the bare faced nerve to ring me and ask me for a reference! I declined.

Now back in the antiques trade, I resolved that this time we would buy *and sell* more items *"in the paint"* - without the hard work of renovations. This I did with many of my new contacts - most of whom had not even been in the trade when I took a break three years before.

We were back on the road! Back in the antiques business which we loved. This would have been around 1988/1989. We maintained and increased our commitment to the antiques trade, which continues still in this year 2020.

Chapter 18
The Re-Launch.

Within a very short space of time, I was back in the deep end of the antiques trade, buying and selling a considerable quantity - mainly antique pine "as found" i.e., unstripped, and hence considerably less labour intensive. I discovered two local dealers in the stripped pine business who I had not met before, indeed they had not been in the job when I moved to Hill View.

Dave Thompson, trading as Laurel Farm, was based in Marsh Lane Longton, in one of the properties which had been on the market during our house search that led us to Hill View. We had dismissed this property as unsuitable and did not even bother to view the interior, simply because of the close proximity of neighbouring properties. As I found out, Dave Thompson had huge amounts of trouble and disputes with the neighbours when he moved in and started working there. His problems with neighbours continued for very many years. Once again, my gut instinct had proved of vital importance.

The other local dealer was Dave Cowell, trading as Country Pine Studio from his shop and home, situated in Much Hoole. It quickly became apparent that these two Dave's were old rivals - in fact, they hated each other. I had to tread a delicate path to deal with both of them.

This hostility between them had gone back to school days. They each had a facility for stripping antique pine furniture, doors, etc, which would be useful to me. They were both very keen to buy from me, as I was managing to obtain some very desirable pieces, having quickly developed a network of new contacts since returning to the pine business.

These contacts included Mohammed, who was situated in Blackburn, and he in turn had access to his many friends and family around the northwest, extending to Manchester. This gave me access to markets which would have otherwise been off limits to me.

Both of the "Daves" were involved in retail selling, so they were not constrained by the pressures of dealing trade to trade, thus enabling me to obtain a higher price than selling to trade-only outlets. In addition, if one Dave thought that the other Dave was likely to be interested in a particularly good item, he was eager to purchase it before the other one spotted it.

Laurel Farm was cashing in on the popularity at that time of "country pine" kitchens - very profitable in itself. He was always willing to pay up, to secure a good or rare item.

Dave Cowell, at Country Pine Studio, was on the other hand keen for me to utilise his shop for retail sales. I provided the stock, Dave did the stripping and waxing, then we shared the profits. Each of them was good to deal with, for one reason or another.

Around that time - some 18 months after selling the milk business - we were hit with a tax enquiry. Inland Revenue were not happy with the percentage profit which we had achieved whilst trading with the milk round.

During the intensive battle to canvas new customers, we had given up to three months free milk, plus we were paying a commission to the salesperson on each of the new housing sites. This had resulted in the profit ratio being about two percent less than that which was expected in the Inland Revenue guidelines. We had achieved an average of thirty-one percent, and their guidelines at that time suggested that it should be thirty-three percent.

Initially, they simply asked for all the old round books, which I had recently burnt. They had been going mouldy and smelt of sour milk, and I had no idea they would be needed. We had our fully documented accounts, verified by our accountant. To me, it was simply a matter of domestic hygiene. To them, it was viewed as destroying evidence.

The result of this was that I was dragged through five different interviews, each very harrowing. Fortunately, I was accompanied to each interview by my accountant, Mr Gaskell. He was extremely experienced in these matters and was quite familiar with all the proceedings, fielding awkward questions with utter brilliance. He viewed them as equals, whereas I viewed them as some sort of God who had enormous power over me. Although I had done nothing wrong, and had not profited in any way in any illegal activity, I felt threatened.

Mr Gaskell revelled in putting these Inland Revenue inspectors "on the back foot". He used no aggression, no hostility, only factual knowledge of the degree of flexibility which he was very much aware that the Inland Revenue would allow. At the conclusion of the fifth meeting, they presented me with a £500 penalty, to which I protested. When we left the meeting, once outside, Mr Gaskell quickly advised me that they must be seen by their superiors to gain something.

He explained to me that the figure they applied as a penalty this year, would also be the amount they would charge for my total income tax bill the following year. That figure (£500) would be my total charge for the full year. I would be quids in. And as an extra bonus, he said that it would not be necessary for him to produce accounts for me for that following year, so I would be saving his normal fee of £300. Mr Gaskell, generously, did not charge me any fee for his preparations for, or attendance at, these five meetings.

So, I agreed - paid HMRC, and got back to the job-in-hand of antique dealing.

However, this was not to be the end of my dealings with the Inland Revenue. As expected, we received a substantial bill for Capital Gains Tax on our sale of the milk round. The figure was in excess of £7,000. But, as Mr Gaskell explained, we could avoid this tax by applying for the "roll-over", which would give us three years to reinvest the gain into another business venture - for example by buying a property from which to trade. This seemed like the best option.

Less than two years into the three-year period, we were startled to get demands for the payment of the tax. Mr Gaskell wrote on our behalf to explain that we were seeking suitable premises from which to trade, and that in his opinion the Inland Revenue were out of order to demand payment before the three years had expired.

Ignoring his letter, they wrote again demanding payment. Mr Gaskell replied - again to no avail. I then received a phone call from a tax-inspector demanding the payment. In the conversation, this person informed me that I could claim the tax back after I had bought the property. I explained that if I paid over the money, I would have insufficient funds to complete the purchase. He insisted that we had to pay.

In sheer panic, I telephoned Mr Gaskell that evening, and although he was about to leave home to attend a dinner party, he took the time to talk to me. He believed that I was being wrongly pursued, and promised to write a strongly worded letter of complaint to the Commissioner for Taxes. The following day he did so, sending us a copy. After this we heard no more from them. We continued our search for a suitable property on New Hall Lane Preston - hoping to recapture our previous success.

Around this time, we had an unexpected visit from Tony Holdsworth, our old customer from Stamford. He had returned from his self-imposed exile in France, and was attempting to claw his way back into the estate agency / property business. We always felt that Tony had been very fair in his dealings with us, and we were pleased to see him. He had several small items of antiques in the boot of his car, which he anxiously asked if we could buy as he needed some cash. We were happy to oblige.

His new wife, Vicky, had taken a small stall in an antique centre in Chester, where they had now settled, but their lack of capital hampered their purchase of stock. We happily agreed a deal whereby we would supply some "finished" pine furniture with which to stock the stall, and they would pay us for it as it sold. This worked very well, with quite a few sales, and we split the profits.

This continued for the best part of a year, when Vicky informed us that the centre had been taken over by one of the dealers within it - Mike Melody. It transpired that Mike had purchased a larger premises in City Road Chester, and was transferring the business to the City Road address. Mike had offered Tony and Vicky a space within this new centre but - although I cannot recall why - they declined. Instead, they offered to put our name forward to replace them if we wanted to, and so we did.

Thus began a period of about eighteen months when we traded out of City Road Chester. Now that we were selling "finished" pine from Chester, we decided that it was time to buy a van. It was easy and convenient to stack up unfinished pine furniture on the pickup, the weather didn't matter - but it was different going to Chester with nicely waxed and polished furniture exposed to the elements.

We purchased a long wheel base Ford Transit. I had become a White Van Man!!!

In the City Road Centre, we were given a large room to share with another pine dealer, Martin. Mike suggested that we just fill the room between us and not worry about dividing the room. This worked out, and although I didn't see Martin very often, we got along well, and the sales were steady.

We were also buying a considerable amount of Belgium furniture made in golden oak (large ornately carved bedroom and dining room suites) from Don Catterell - a dealer originally from Blackpool. Don was the brother-in-law of Colin Robinson, the dealer in Hull from whom we had previously bought vast quantities of pine furniture. We took a few of these suites down to the centre in Chester, as well as the stripped pine. All was well, until Martin decided to leave following an argument with Mike, the owner of the centre.

The next time I went down to Chester, Mike had leased the large room to another dealer, and we had been allocated a small booth measuring only about eight feet by six feet, and our furniture was all just piled up higgledy-piggledy. I was not impressed! I decided to leave, but had to give three months notice. We made quite a few sales during this period, but they were always heavily discounted by Mike. I took leave of Chester with no regrets.

The next outlet which I took on was a new venture that had opened at a disused mill in Eccleston, trading as Bygone Times. The company was advertising for stall holders at a very attractive rent, providing you paid for a year in advance. By taking advantage of this offer it worked out at about £12 per week.

We took up residence, and remained there for a total of eight years, during which time we achieved some very reasonable sales. With such an attractive offer, the building quickly filled and so more space in the building was opened up.

The downside of this popularity meant that there were a huge number of part-time dealers, mostly retired, who were able to spend a great deal of time there, and it became hugely competitive.

We also resumed our visits to Park Hall Antiques Fair, which was held on Sunday mornings. We had ceased exhibiting at this fair a few years earlier, whilst we were so busy with our shops and supplying Handsome Pine in Stamford. We now visited Park Hall Fair as potential buyers, rather than sellers, and discovered that it had expanded considerably since our last visits. It now consisted of a huge outdoor market starting very early (around 4am), as well as the indoor fair with which we were familiar, which started at 8am.

I decided to make this a regular call on Sunday mornings, often accompanied by Stephen when he was on his alternate weekend visits home from Up Holland College.

My first foray into this large outdoor selling space soon made me realise that this was also extremely competitive, with aggressive buyers rushing to surround each new arrival, elbowing other dealers out of their way to get "first dibs" on any bargains. Getting my hands on any good pine was going to be pretty difficult.

Stephen and I, not having bought anything during the first half hour, came across a large pile of mouth-watering pine furniture, stacked around a van behind the main stands.

We looked with envy! This was where I first met Bernard.

Bernard, I learned, was there from around 3.30am, before the first sellers even arrived on the scene. He was the champion of "getting in first" and woe betide anybody who tried to beat him to it. His method was to leap on any approaching van or car, and then cling on until the vehicle stopped at its allocated pitch, then he bounded to the ground and guarded the doors, so he was first there.

As we gazed at this pile of good stock, Bernard returned with even more bounty.

'Is this yours?' I enquired. He replied that it was.
He asked me 'What do you want? Something cheap, I expect.'
'Not necessarily' I replied.

With this response, Bernard's mood mellowed. We soon got along fine! Bernard was as sharp as a razor, but not greedy.

I discovered that everything he bought was for resale. He had such a vast array of contacts, and was buying not just pine - but across the entire antique spectrum. With his aggressive manner of buying, he was probably able to get the items cheaper than I could.

I soon worked out that, rather than trying to compete in this crazy scrum that was the buying mania in those heady days of antique dealing, it was better for me to let Bernard do the buying. Even with his margin added, I was able to buy my selected items at a more reasoned pace - and still at a competitive price.

We soon established a very good trade relationship, and I continued to deal with Bernard for very many years.

My approach to buying only the best quality furniture was to view the inside and underneath of surfaces, to ensure that items were properly constructed, with no inferior wood or plywood. To this end, I always removed at least one drawer to allow a detailed inspection. Stephen was well trained in this, and on one memorable occasion, whilst examining a prospective purchase from Bernard, Stephen removed the drawer and, looking underneath the lining, discovered pinned to the bottom a bundle of banknotes.

Quicker than a terrier down a rat hole, Bernard was on it. 'Well done lad' he exclaimed, and swiftly grabbed the notes from Stephen, and stuffed them in his pocket.

Our reward for this find was a £5 reduction on the asking price of the chest of drawers, which I felt obligated to give to Stephen as a reward for his diligence. On our return home that day, Stephen went through our own considerable stock of furniture, searching every single drawer and cupboard for more loot, but to no avail.

One thing this did teach me was to examine future purchases more discreetly.

A few months later, whilst thoroughly examining a chest of drawers at an auction room, having removed the top drawer I spotted a bundle of banknotes pinned to the underside of the top, and hastily replaced the drawer. I leant up against the chest for the duration of the sale in an attempt to hide the booty from other viewers, and did not dare to leave it unguarded. Determined to buy it, I paid some £10 or £20 over the usual price to secure it. As soon as the sale had completed, with the assistance of another dealer, I removed it immediately. When I got it home and examined it at my leisure, I found a total of more than £400.

My regular visits to the Sunday morning market at Park Hall also produced many other useful contacts and customers, including quite a few overseas buyers who came to England regularly - particularly when the Newark International fairs were on, which was six times a year. These included Maria's Antiques from California, and a group of three friends trading from Maine, USA, and Mark Crumpler from Carolina, as well as UK buyers such as Roger Haynes from Leek, and many more. All of these were regular buyers, to whom we continued to sell for many years.

During this time, Newark Fair was one of the highlights of the antique dealers' calendar, but I had never visited it during the early years - being far too busy with the demanding physical effort and time of stripping and refurbishing huge amounts of pine furniture. But when I developed a friendship with a fellow stallholder at Bygone Times, Keith Blackburn, the opportunity to visit Newark Fair came to be.

Following a morning at Warren and Wignalls saleroom, Keith would come back to our house for lunch. During our chats it transpired that he went to Newark on his own, staying for both days, stopping overnight in his tent. He obviously enjoyed it, but was not really keen on going on his own. He had been medically retired from his job as an engineer after suffering several heart attacks, the first when he was only 32 years old.

At this point in time, our son Kevin had left his job as a shop manager and had come to work full time with me. This allowed me a little more free time, so it was decided that I would accompany Keith to the next Newark Fair. Keith still took his little tent, and I slept in the van. We took some stock with us, did a bit of selling, and a lot of buying, with frequent returns to the van for brews and bacon butties, which we made on our little camping stove. It was generally a lot of fun, and I know Keith enjoyed it. It was successful enough for us to return to all the fairs for the following year. On a few occasions, Kevin came along also.

Kevin and I also visited the Furniture Show at the NEC in Birmingham several times. Kevin thought that it would be nice to invite Keith along (we were the happy recipients of free tickets). Keith was keen to go with us, and would have enjoyed the day out, but the next Furniture Show coincided with his wife's birthday, so he declined on that occasion.

Kevin and I went to the show, had a very enjoyable but exhausting day, and arrived home around 7pm. Imagine my shock when I received a phone call at 7.30pm from Keith's wife, Joan, telling me that Keith had collapsed and died around lunch time that day.

Keith had been a great friend with whom we had shared some great laughs. He was a very quiet and unassuming man, and only forty-one years old when he died. Joan later told me how much he had enjoyed his trips out with Kevin and myself. We were just so glad that he did not come to the furniture show that day; at least he was at home with Joan when he died.

Kevin and I went to his funeral, as did several other dealers from Bygone Times. We undertook to remove all his stock and put it in Warren and Wignalls auction on Joan's behalf. This was a great relief to her, and it was the least we could do for a good friend and his widow.

We continued to attend Newark fairs, accompanied by various children! Sometimes Maggie came, sometimes Alison, often Kevin, as this was now his full-time job.

To counteract the competition to sell pine furniture at Bygone Times, we developed a new strategy by trading in superb-quality, excellent-value-for-money, dining room and bedroom furniture in oak and walnut, which was imported from the Continent. We purchased these from a dealer friend, Don Catterall, who made trips to Europe at least once a month and returned with his van and roof rack fully laden.

Don's visits to us became quite an event. He would arrive at our house in the morning and stay all day, quickly learning that Cathy's hospitality meant that he could have his lunch and his dinner with us, and countless cups of tea and homemade cakes - often not leaving until late in the evening.

The continental suites of furniture were a real hit at Bygone Times. We would regularly sell a suite the same day that we placed it on the stall.

During this era at Bygone Times, another very significant development took place - we finally found shop premises to purchase. Although I had reservations about doing so, it was necessary to enact the "roll over" of capital gains tax profit from the sale of the milk round. Neither of us relished handing more than £7,000 to the tax man.

The property we decided to acquire was in New Hall Lane, but it was further out of town from where we had been before (New Hall Lane is about two miles long). It had previously been a shoe repair shop, and the asking price of £32,000 was the cheapest commercial property we had found anywhere. The advice from Mr Gaskell, our accountant, was to re-mortgage our house, Hill View, thus benefiting from a lower rate of interest than a commercial mortgage would have been.

As the three-year period allowed for the tax rollover was coming to an end, we needed to action a quick purchase in order to avoid any further confrontation with the Inland Revenue. With this in mind, we short-term borrowed the purchase money from Cathy's brother, Eddie, who willingly advanced the £32,000 required, and declined any offer of interest. He was visiting us at the time these negotiations were going on, and he offered to help. Once the purchase was complete, we were able, with the accountant's help, to re-mortgage Hill View and thus repay Eddie very quickly.

Once we took possession of the shop, we began the mammoth task of bringing it up to a reasonable standard as quickly as possible, so that we could open it as a retail premise for our antique furniture. We paid out to get the roof and gutters sorted, and the back kitchen was improved with a new sink unit. From the start, I realised that the remaining work was going to be a huge undertaking, taking many hours even to just remove old wallpaper from the front saleroom before we were able to redecorate. After long hours of painstaking work, we managed to get the downstairs area of the shop ready for opening.

When we did finally open, although we made some sales, we began to realise that we were not going to repeat the success of earlier years in the other (rented) shop on New Hall Lane. Eventually, with the help of Stephen, our friend Pete Kelly, and Ken (our future son-in-law) and others, we completed the renovation and made the upstairs usable as well. We were still in Bygone Times at this time, and tried to direct customers from our display there to our shop in New Hall Lane, but with limited success.

During these last few years (the mid 1980's to 1990) our youngest son Stephen had been, as already mentioned, residing as a boarder at St Joseph's College, Up Holland. This had previously been a boarding school and seminary for the training of young men for the priesthood. It had closed as a boarding school in the mid 1980's, but one wing of the college remained open for boarding young men who still expressed an interest in training for the priesthood. Their education was now done off-site, at the local Catholic school.

Whilst living in this vast and lovely old property, Stephen and his newfound friends were allowed to explore the amazing huge premises, which was now mostly empty of people. The only occupants were Stephen and his friends, eight in total, together with the lovely priest who looked after them, Father Cunningham, and Father Bouchard - who administered the building.

Stephen's discovery of old dormitories full of furniture, together with his enthusiasm to help me in my antique business, led to another exciting chapter of events.

Chapter 19
Up Holland and Beyond.

Stephen and his group of friends at St Joseph's College Up Holland explored this enormous and impressive gothic style building, built in the 1880's, at their leisure. They were free to roam wherever they wished.

Stephen's first year there coincided with the sale of the milk business and the resumption of antique dealing. He had accompanied me during his pre-school years to many antique shops, and he was well aware that this historic building contained many items with mouth-watering appeal. On his visits home, he related with some enthusiasm what he had come across, and thus whetted my appetite.

Having secured permission from the priest in charge of the building, Father Bouchard, when I went to collect Stephen for one of his regular visits home, he showed me just a few of the rooms that he had discovered. All were eerily quiet, and the contents of the rooms and dormitories were exactly as they had been left after the departure of the last boarders.

It was indeed, from an antique dealer's perspective, mouth-watering.

There were wardrobes, cupboards, bedside lockers, mahogany chests of drawers, dozens of Victorian kitchen chairs, and much more. Most of this furniture dated from the end of the 19th century. A lot of it was of pine construction, which was right up my street. I was definitely interested if they were selling.

Stephen informed Father Bouchard of my interest, but he was not receptive. He told Stephen that he had been bombarded with, and had fended off, many requests from dealers to get into the building ever since the news came out that the college was closing.

Eventually, Father Bouchard agreed to meet with me.

His knowledge of us was that we had a milk business - he was not aware of our previous history and substantial knowledge of antiques, and was therefore very sceptical. In the end, it was agreed that I could submit prices for items that I could be interested in buying.

There were many "repeat items" which were virtually identical, so I offered a fixed price per unit, regardless of condition. For example, kitchen chairs at £10 each - covering some that were in good condition, and some that were badly damaged but could potentially be used for spare parts. Quite a few had had a hard life, consistent with use by hundreds of boys over more than a hundred years, with missing spindles etc. For each chest of drawers, we offered £50, and for each cupboard, £30 and so on, again regardless of condition.

At this point in the proceedings, Father Bouchard raised his hands. 'Stop!', he said.

I thought that we were being rejected, but to my utter surprise he said, 'At those prices, you can begin by clearing the dormitories, and we will see how we go on from there. In your own time, as soon as you are ready.'

I was delighted.

Anxious to prove my integrity, I labelled each item with a number so that I was able to give him a list of what we took each time: a price for each item and the total, accompanied by a cheque.

There was a huge amount of furniture to be cleared and a lot of physical work involved, as there were five flights of stairs to the dormitories and a further two flights to the attic rooms. It was too great a task for Cathy and me to handle on our own. I enlisted the help of Dave Cowell. At this time Dave and I were working together a lot, and I was using his pine stripping facilities regularly - at least once a week. Dave was delighted to be given the opportunity to be involved in such an interesting and potentially rewarding venture.

Generally, we went to the college every Tuesday, returning with two vehicles filled to maximum capacity including the roof racks. Over several months we cleared the dormitories and moved on to the attic rooms.

We sold quite a lot of the furniture as we went along - some at Dave's shop, some into the trade, and some at Bygone Times where we each had a stall. We paid very fair prices relative to the market at that time, and made a conscious decision from the beginning to pay the same price for each piece where there were multiples, whether in good condition or damaged. This way we figured we could repair some of the damaged items using spares from others.

This method also made it very straight forward when producing a list of what we were taking to give to Father Buchard. So, every cupboard, or *part cupboard*, was £50. Every chest of drawers, or *part of a chest of drawers*, was £30. And so on.

It was after we had cleared a few of the incomplete cupboards from a storeroom, and then moved to some attic rooms, that we found some similar part-cupboards. We began to consider if it was possible that some of these pieces belonged together. We put these incomplete items in our store, and some months later we attempted to get them all together. Sure enough, there were four units which clearly had originally been one - forming an extremely large and rare bedroom combination unit. It also incorporated a washstand with a marble top, complete with sixteen Minton tiles forming part of the structure.

There was some damage, and sections of moulding were missing, but over several weeks we stripped, repaired, and assembled this enormous piece of furniture. Our son, Kevin, very expertly replaced the parts of the missing moulding using the original bits as a template, and did such an excellent job that no one, no matter how experienced a dealer / restorer, could ever point out which parts had been replaced.

One of my regular trade buyers at that time, Will - trading as Utopia Pine in Cumbria, offered us £1,250 pounds for the cupboard when he saw it partly finished. Unfortunately, my colleague Dave saw this as an indication that it was worth an absolute fortune, and insisted that he would put it on his stall in Bygone Times for £4,000, a figure which I considered to be truly ridiculous! It certainly attracted a huge amount of interest, including from John Rigby, who was the owner of Bygone Times at that time. But no sale resulted.

In the end, it sat there for months and months. After a long time, I finally managed to prise it away from Dave and put it in the shop which we had bought on New Hall Lane. Again, no sale resulted.

When we closed the shop a couple of years later, another pine dealer, Hadyn Lathom, who at that time was based at Blackpool, offered to put it in his shop. Once again, it was to remain there until some two years later when he moved from the shop.

At this point we were invited to put it on display in Paul Allison's warehouse, which he had recently opened in Leyland. It did not sell there either!

Eventually we put it into storage in Kevin's workshop in Bold Street Preston, where it remained for another few years.

Finally, probably nearly twenty years after we originally acquired it, the "College Piece" as it had become known was relegated to Warren and Wignalls auction room in Leyland, where it realised £700.

The moral here is... the first profit is always the best, so take it. Such a large item was not suited for most homes and required a very specific type of buyer.

Over a number of months, we spent in excess of £5,000 at St Joseph's. Father Buchard had seemed well pleased with the funds raised. He indicated that when we had finished in this part at the rear of the building, he wanted us to start on the rooms at the front, which had been the bishops and priests' accommodation. These of course were furnished with good quality and comfortable furniture, and were a far cry from the austere and basic items which we had been clearing from the dormitories.

However, this was not to be.

Father Buchard suddenly called a halt to our clearance. We never really knew why as he offered us no explanation. A couple of years later, I spotted a few of the easily recognizable chest of drawers from the college at Preston Antique Centre. They were on the stall of a dealer who was, by day, a schoolteacher at a catholic secondary school - the antique dealing being for him a part-time venture. He was renowned for being tight-fisted in his dealings and always wanting high profits. I also saw more of the very identifiable pieces of furniture with a dealer in Cumbria, who confirmed to me that he had bought them from the said dealer in Preston.

On one of my visits to Preston Antique Centre, I broached the subject of Up Holland with the schoolteacher / dealer, who aggressively made it clear to me that he thought he had more right to the college job than we did - because he was a teacher in a catholic school! This confirmed my suspicions. When we had been thrown off the job very abruptly and without explanation, it was the result of a thorough character assassination by this bitter man. We never found out what had been said, but it must have been very bad indeed.

This same part-time dealer had previously lambasted me for having the audacity to leave bids on pine furniture at an auction in Lytham. He considered that this auction was "his" for buying, and told me in no uncertain terms that if I wanted to buy at this auction, I had to do it through him. He wanted paying out. In other words - join his "ring".

The ring is when several dealers get together and negotiate the price of a lot, so they don't bid against each other. One of the ring members is nominated to do the buying in the auction, ensuring that he is the only bidder, thus crippling the price that the vendor will receive. At the conclusion of the sale, the dealers get together and have a mini auction between themselves. The winner of this auction gets to keep the item, and the difference between the two costs is put into a pot and shared out between them.

In those days, the practice of "the ring", which I have always found abhorrent, was a well-established and common practice in almost all auction rooms throughout the country. It was, and still is, illegal.

I have always fiercely resisted any invitation to join any ring, in any auction room. It was not only illegal but immoral. The principle of any auction is that the item up for sale goes to the highest bidder. I resented the idea that any other dealer would dictate to me what I was allowed to buy, and then to add insult to injury by demanding money from me for the privilege.

As far as the St Joseph's clearance was concerned, we had a clear conscience. We had paid good and fair prices, and did a very tidy job of removal. During the period of removal, we had been informed by the caretaker, who was always present to assist and check what was being removed, that Father Bouchard had previously been offered a *best* bid of 50p per chair, whereas we had paid £10 for every chair, even if damaged - and we were still able to make a profit. Whatever had been said and by whom to cause the premature termination of our agreement, we had no cause for regret in terms of any of our own actions.

For me, that job was not just about the money. It was fascinating to be allowed to roam this vast historic building, now largely unused, which had been home for many hundreds of trainee priests over the course of almost a century. The "Long Corridor" (228 feet) to the main chapel was lined by group photographs of each year's attendees, and a large majority of boys who attended this school did go on to be ordained into the priesthood.

The scale of St. Josephs was such that its Quad, at nearly an acre in size, was much larger than any to be found within any colleges at Oxford or Cambridge University. The demand for applications to this calling had once been so great, that during the war years the attics were converted to accommodate seminarians fleeing Nazi Europe.

It is interesting to note that Mr Phillip Warren, one of the founders of Warren and Wignalls auction room, told me that he had attended St Joseph's Up Holland himself as a trainee priest, but decided to pursue a different career.

So, Up Holland and working closely with Dave became another step, leading us to our next adventure.

Chapter 20
London Calling.

I had recently subscribed to the 'Antiques Trade Gazette'.

A few weeks after we had finished at Up Holland, whilst eagerly reading the latest edition, I spotted an advertisement for space to rent in a London antique centre.

I thought this worthy of some consideration, and I shared my thoughts with Dave Cowell when we were next working together at his workshop. Dave was a time-served painter and decorator, and he told me that one of his contracts had involved working for some time in London. He had enjoyed being there, and was familiar with the area where this antique centre was located. He suggested that we take a fact-finding trip to investigate further.

The advert was for space within Penny Farthing Antiques in Bermondsey, just south of the river and very close to Tower Bridge. We made an appointment with the owner to meet at the centre. A very early start was required, the journey down taking almost five hours. Peter, the owner, was very friendly and down to earth. He showed us the available pitch, gave us all the information regarding the cost etc. and gave us very helpful advice about what was selling well in the location at that time.

We had managed to park quite close to the antique centre on a parking meter, and made good use of the remaining time by quickly scouring the neighbourhood, which we found to be a little hub of antique shops and centres. We quickly ascertained the going price of items for sale. We realised that, at the prices being asked, we could easily make decent profits. We returned to Penny Farthing Antiques immediately, and promptly signed the lease agreement with Peter.

By coincidence, we learnt that the outgoing tenant, whose pitch we were taking over, was a person I knew well. He was a dealer from Liverpool who also had space at the Preston Antique Centre, and he was moving out of Penny Farthing to take up a bigger stand just around the corner at Tower Bridge Antiques.

It's a small world!!!

We moved into Penny Farthing, which was quite a small centre, but the owner Peter was very enthusiastic and helpful. The space we had taken on was in the basement and accessed down a very tight and bendy staircase, but as there were the two of us, the stairs were no problem.

There was a very healthy overseas trade in that area at the time, and we were to discover that our mixture of antique stripped pine and the usual array of other Victorian furniture went down well. A very popular seller, which we discovered by chance, was Victorian and 1920's/30's furniture (such as chest of drawers, blanket chests, occasional tables) which had been painted with a nautical theme, such as ships, charts, telescopes etc. These were hand painted by another of our old friend Bernard's contacts, and they went down a storm (not literally) in London.

We had planned to do a trip to London every other Tuesday as a routine, but would very often receive a call from Peter by the end of the first week to say that our stand was almost empty, and asking when we could return with more stock. It reminded me in many ways of the vigour in our trade that we had experienced when we first started to supply Handsome Pine in Stamford some ten years earlier.

We also enjoyed making new contacts in the Bermondsey area. For example, another stall holder at Penny Farthing, when he saw that we had a collection of pine furniture, asked if we would be interested in buying unstripped (painted pine), as he regularly did house clearances and was looking for an outlet for such items. This was ideal, as it meant that we made a profit from the return journey also. He was a very interesting character - a London taxi driver in the evenings and at weekends, with business cards in the back of his cab advertising his house clearance business.

Each time we arrived to unload in Bermondsey Street, we attracted the attention of dealers from other adjacent emporiums, who would descend on our van to get "first dibs" at the fresh stock arriving.

One of these became a very regular customer. He had a large warehouse in a street adjacent to Penny Farthing, and asked if we could telephone him the day before we came, so that he could be on hand to take his pick.

So, it became the norm that we would call both this customer and our taxi driver friend, and thus a good day's trading was ensured for us all.

Once we had unloaded, and in turn loaded any items we bought onto the van, we adjourned to a superb little cafe further down Bermondsey Street, owned by an Italian lady who served up a fabulous roast dinner for very little money. We would then set off on the long journey back home. Happy Days!!!!!

There was one particularly memorable return journey. As we were leaving the centre, we were advised about a storm warning which had just been broadcast on the radio. As we exited Bermondsey Street, things were already blowing about wildly. We had only just got across Tower Bridge when it became apparent that the traffic was already in chaos, and many roads were already blocked by falling debris.

When we finally got as far as the Edgware Road, we came across a Luton van which had been blown over on its side as it travelled between two tall buildings. A few days later, we were to discover that the van belonged to our dealer friend and previous owner of our stand in Penny Farthing, Carl Yates. Fortunately, Carl was unhurt.

When we did finally reach the M1 to continue our exit from London, conditions did not improve. We came across many more high-sided vehicles which had been blown over in this ferocious storm. It took us more than eight hours to get home, but we made it safely.

Peter offered us additional space in Penny Farthing when an adjacent unit became available, which we took. We learned a very valuable lesson then: we doubled our rent costs, but did not significantly increase our sales. Over time, from this centre and in other outlets, I discovered that increasing the size of a pitch does not substantially increase the income that it generates. It is far better to take a second pitch but in a different location - even if that second location is still within the same centre. This is something I have since practised over the years, and still do now in 2020.

By reading advertisements in trade publications, we sought out other dealers we could purchase from, in order to make our return journeys from London even more cost effective. The first avenue we followed was an antique centre in Luton, which although itself was not fruitful it led us to discover a small second-hand shop, run by a couple whose roots were in Wales, where they sourced regular house clearances. This contact proved to be very lucrative for us.

Soon, we were regularly cramming our van full on every return trip from London - mainly, at that time, with bedroom suites from the 1920/30's era. By the following day, this furniture would be on my pitch in the Preston Antique Centre on New Hall Lane, where it mostly sold within a few days - often to Paul Allison, the owner of that centre. Paul was, at that time, a 'shipper' and was sending furniture in containers across the waves to his contacts all over America.

During these busy and exciting times, we developed several other useful "stop-offs" to combine with our London trips. The next dealer we decided to investigate was Clover Antiques, at Fordham near Newmarket.

It was relatively easy to leave London via the M11 and detour to Newmarket. Our first visit was memorable! His trading address was his home, with several timber buildings and stables in his fields. The buildings were full of joinery machinery, where he had begun a business manufacturing reproduction furniture, some of which was quite complicated to make, such as circular Art Deco style display cabinets. Not the easiest thing to reproduce - we were impressed!!

The owner, Martin, was welcoming, but to be honest - he looked menacing. The impression I got was that you would not want to cross him. He informed us that his pine operation was located at a farm a few miles away, and he invited us to go there. He said he would lead the way and we were to follow. As he sped off in his Range Rover, we followed behind in our van, feeling slightly jealous of his luxurious transport.

The farm was "in the middle of nowhere", a complex of barns and outbuildings, but once inside - the scene was memorising. Martin definitely knew what he was about. He had the most impressive set up for door stripping that either Dave or I had ever seen.

A large stripping tank, probably five meters square, was sunk into the floor with a huge, specially designed metal crate to hold about fifty doors in individual spaces. The whole thing was then lowered into the tank by an electric hoist. He was stripping doors on an industrial scale for several builders / property restorers who were working on period properties in the area. It was clearly a money spinner, processing (as he told us) hundreds of doors a week, but it had required a significant investment.

Using the profits from the door stripping, he was now developing the furniture manufacturing business, mainly from oak, as well as those complicated cabinets and more.

By now, we were warming to Martin. He certainly did not do things by half. He took us to another area of the building, where the furniture that we had actually come to see (continental pine) was stored. Martin's prices were fair, so we quickly purchased six large sectional wardrobes.

The three of us stacked them all outside, ready to pack in the van. Martin locked the door of the barn. 'Right lads' he said, 'see you back at home.' And he was gone!!!

No money had changed hands.

Attempts to get these new purchases into the van, which was already half full, proved impossible. We decided that the only option was to unload completely and start again from scratch. It was a summer evening, still very hot, at the end of a long day, and we still had a long journey home. But after a long, sweaty hour or so of hard graft, all was loaded safely with room to spare.

As we set off back to Martin's base, we half expected to see him appear on the horizon in hot pursuit of the pair of us. He must have pondered whether we had "done a runner" without paying. He had never met us before that day, he had no idea what sort of people we were, and he had no idea where we had come form, or where we were going back to. No mobile phones in those days! Our original perception of Martin was that it would be a brave man who would attempt such a thing.

When we eventually arrived back at his house to pay him and get a cup of tea, he really didn't seem bothered. We must have looked honest! His looks belied the fact that he was a grand person to deal with, and honourable. We returned on several occasions.

It was approaching midnight when we finally reached home. We had set off at 4am. Another very long day, which many antiques dealers will know is not unusual, as we travel far and wide scouring the country to find stock. But we all love it, or we wouldn't do it!!!

Martin eventually gave up dealing in old pine and concentrated on further developing the Clover brand of high-quality reproduction furniture. We spotted him some time later at the Furniture Show at the NEC in Birmingham - where he had an impressive display, and again when visiting Newark Antique Fair - where he was exhibiting his furniture from a mobile showroom, which he had converted very successfully from a large horse box. As I have said, he did not do things by half-measure.

Our frequent journeys to London gave us the opportunity to seek out more dealers in the south who we could visit on our regular journeys home. To this end, we sought out another pine dealer who advertised in the trade publications - Barry Sykes and his two sons, who traded near Brandy Wharf in the Lincolnshire Wolds.

They were also operating from a barn complex, miles from anywhere! It was pure luck that we managed to find them at all when we first visited. There was a huge barn with a dirt floor containing row upon row of mouth-watering continental / European pine furniture of good quality. We did a considerable amount of buying from them on this and many subsequent occasions. However, they did have a habit of frequently moving premises.

Their last move was to a purpose-built unit, which they had designed and erected on a piece of land which Barry had bought from British Rail. The express trains flew past at such a speed that we often had to stop speaking to each other until they had hurtled past the building. This was very frequent.

By this time, Barry had bought a home in France and left the running of the pine business in England to his two sons, whom I dealt with for many years. In later times, when my travelling companion Dave Cowell was no longer working in the antique business, I would continue to buy from Barry's sons.

Occasionally Barry himself would be there, and he amused himself and our two girls, Alison and Maggie, by speaking to them in French. They were about twelve and ten by this point. Our children were with us whenever possible on our trips around the country. This was a wonderful bonus, and their company was something that money could never buy.

We often struck horror into the owners of antique shops, especially those trading in rare and expensive ceramics, when we appeared through their doors, in our early days, with four very small children in tow! And in later years, there were often six children in tow. However, we were welcomed by all - as soon as we had established that we were serious buyers.

Back at Penny Farthing in Bermondsey, after Dave had left antique dealing to pursue a different career, I was delighted to continue the business there with my good friend Paul Norris. However, times were changing (again) in the antique business. As always, our business was dictated by trends and fashions; these changed dramatically and suddenly, and for the last three months of trading from Penny Farthing we only sold one item of furniture. This was in stark contrast to the fervent activity to which we had become accustomed.

So, with regret, we left Penny Farthing Antiques.

This period of being in London, and all that it entailed, was one of the most enjoyable times that we have had, and certainly the busiest.

We did return to dealing in London the following year, when trade improved again, but this time on our own. I took a space in Tower Bridge Antiques, just a few hundred yards from the bridge itself. It was a large space on the third floor of the building.

The furniture would be loaded onto a forklift, the staff would raise it to the required height, and then begin a very precarious procedure to unload it. This involved removing part of the protective rail around the walkway on the third floor, in order to place the furniture onto our pitch. Health and Safety would have a field day!!!! Fortunately, no accidents occurred. At that time, the tenants in Tower Bridge Antiques also included Brett Griffiths (West Lancs. Antiques) and Carl Yates, both from our part of the world.

We stayed at Tower Bridge Antiques until other avenues and opportunities beckoned. Our time in London was interesting, exciting, profitable, and brought us into contact with many wonderful characters. I wouldn't have swapped it for the world!!!

Chapter 21
Changing Times.

The period of the early 1990's saw the opening of the shop that we had purchased in New Hall Lane Preston, following the sale of the milk business. As previously mentioned, it was clear that we were not going to achieve great success from that shop, like that we had experienced the first time around on New Hall Lane. Times they were indeed a-changing.

We did however achieve considerable business successes through our contacts – old and new.

The first part of this decade, whilst I was working alongside Dave Cowell, brought several very useful contacts via Bygone Times.

The first of these, Geoffrey Pitt - trading as Pine Finds from his base near Ripon in North Yorkshire, had come to Dave's shop following a visit to Bygone Times. He bought a couple of pieces of furniture which had been supplied by me.

Dave was not so used to dealing with large quantities as I was - his shop was a retail business rather than servicing trade customers. When Dave realised that Geoffrey was a "big fish" who was looking to buy in large quantity, he brought him the couple of miles up the road to visit me at Hill View.

At that time, I had several hundred pieces of furniture stacked in barns and outbuildings, some "ready to go" but most were in the original Victorian paint. Geoffrey was clearly impressed, and proceeded to order a large number of items from the stock I held, but he wanted it all to be stripped and polished prior to delivery. Dave and I both worked extremely hard over the subsequent three weeks until the order was ready for delivery. We set off towards Ripon with two large vans crammed full of furniture.

When we arrived at Pine Finds it quickly became obvious that Geoffrey was not going to buy anything like the amount that he had ordered. All the items were finished to our usual high standard, and I was in no doubt at all that if Geoffrey did not buy it, we could easily sell it elsewhere. Eventually he picked and poked through the items, and finished up buying about two thirds of what he had originally ordered.

Pine Finds was selling mainly export, in large quantities, and with hindsight I am convinced that he had experienced some sort of problem with his overseas customers. It was so common for dealers who exported huge quantities - sending many container loads of furniture with the assurance that payment was on the way, only to subsequently discover that payment was inexplicably delayed.

I continued to deal with Geoffrey, but with smaller orders and quantities. By now, Dave had moved on to pastures new. On one occasion, Geffrey asked me to pick up some items from a dealer on the Wirral, and deliver them to his base at Ripon when I came with his next order - and he would pay me for my time.

The Wirral dealer was someone I was slightly familiar with from my days in the antique centre in Chester, he certainly knew me. He telephoned to give me directions on how to find him; he was another dealer working from a barn in a remote rural area, not easy to locate.

It was a beautiful summer day, and Alison and Maggie came along with me for the ride. After loading Geffrey's items onto the van, I was offered a cup of coffee and a chat. It was a lovely rural location and the girls asked if they could play outside. I considered that this was no problem, and the dealer pointed out that there were no roads to the rear of his property, just open fields, and a bridle way.

After about twenty minutes, as I prepared to take my leave, I went outside and there was no sight nor sound of the girls. The whole area was very open, and you could see for about a mile or more across the fields. I called, then shouted. When yelling at the top of my voice still brought no response, the panic set in.

I set off running along the bridle way. When I reached a sort of crossroads where divergent paths went off into the fields, I had no idea which way to go next, so I decided to keep straight on towards a slight ridge, where hopefully I could see further down the other side. When I reached the top, I could see a group of walkers far away in the distance, and wondered if they might have seen the girls.

I ran down the path after them, yelling frantically in an attempt to catch their attention. As I drew nearer, I could see two little figures trailing behind the walkers - I realised it was them!!! Still yelling, I managed to get someone to hear me, and the group stopped.

The little rascals then started back towards me. It turned out that, as they were playing outside the dealer's barn, the ramblers came strolling past, and they (I suspect Alison as she is the more adventurous) decided that it would be great fun to go walkies with them! The ramblers each assumed that the girls belonged to someone else in the group. I will never forget the feeling of panic when I realised that they were not outside the barn where I had left them playing.

The girls were with me again a few days later when I made the delivery to Geoffrey. They made quite an impression on him. He had advertising mugs printed with the name of his business and a picture of his premises, and proceeded to give the girls a mug each, which we still have. Afterwards I took the girls into Ripon for a sightseeing walkabout, but this time I never let them out of my sight!

I continued to deal with Geffrey Pitt at Pine Finds until his unexpected and sudden death the following year.

During this period, there was no shortage of small shops offering antique stripped pine, which was hugely fashionable, and they all required regular supplies of stock. This was our speciality, and although we had retail premises ourselves, my focus was to obtain regular trade customers.

One such customer who found us, again via Bygone Times, was Dave Gibbons (nearly every pine dealer seemed to be called Dave). This Dave hailed from Henley-on-Thames, and his shop there attracted quite a few celebrity customers. At that time, his shop was seen by discerning, wealthy customers as "The Place" to buy antique pine. Dave later informed me that his customers who purchased items of pine that I had supplied included Steve Wright and the late Terry Wogan, both from Radio Two, amongst others.

Dave also had a shop in Windsor, and another in Maidstone. Initially, for a period of about two years or so, Dave would come to us to choose and collect what he wanted to buy. With the progression of time, he concentrated on his shop in Windsor, and as he had developed an increasing trust in my selection of items suitable for his customers, he simply rang and placed an order. We would deliver directly to Windsor for him. This shop was positioned in an excellent retail position on the historic High Street, which led directly up to the stunning Windsor Castle.

By this time, I was also dealing with Tony from Yesterday's Pine in Eastleigh, near Southampton, who I was introduced to when a customer of mine recommended me to him. It was relatively easy to deliver to Windsor and then travel on to Eastleigh via the M4 and the M27, and thus I was able to deliver a van full of goods to Windsor, then proceed with the empty van to purchase more stock at Eastleigh - resulting in a very economical day's trading.

The return journey was often a nightmare, especially on a Friday, when it would take at least an hour just to get through Newbury, until a year or so later when they finally opened the Newbury Bypass.

On one particular day, when I arrived at the Windsor shop around 10am, his normal opening time, there was a middle-aged "arty-looking" lady in his shop. She looked more than a little anxious, and Dave was clearly also anxious (to be rid of her). It transpired that Dave was having piano lessons, and she was his teacher. She had gone to the theatre somewhere nearby the previous evening, had missed her last train home, and in panic she had phoned Dave, knowing that he lived in Windsor. He had very kindly put her up for the night. She desperately needed to get to her home in Ascot, but he was reluctant to close the shop to take her there. I was going down the M4, in that general direction (?!) so my help was enlisted to take the lady home.

She was very charming, but I am sure that she did not relish the idea of being stuck in a van with a complete stranger either. I safely delivered this lovely lady to her home, and proceeded on my way to Eastleigh. A knight in shining armour!

We next sought out a pine shop in Cambridge, trading as The Pine Merchant.

A few years prior to mum's death, mum and dad had moved from our house in Grantchester to sheltered accommodation in Girton. This was nearer to my aunt Doreen, who at that time lived alone. When Doreen subsequently remarried and moved away, my parents felt somewhat isolated, and now after mum had died, and dad was on his own, I knew that he was anxious to return to Grantchester.

Through the local council he was able to obtain a transfer to sheltered accommodation, back in Grantchester. Stephen and I spent a hectic weekend moving him and all his possessions.

We had discovered The Pine Merchant shop near the English Martyrs Church in Cambridge, where we attended Mass on the weekends that we went to visit dad. The shop was always closed on Sundays, but an appraisal through the windows of the stock on offer was enough to confirm in our minds that we could potentially do some business.

We decided to visit the shop during opening hours, so on our next visit to dad we called at the Pine Merchant - armed with photos of our own stock, a list of prices, and made ourselves known to the owner, Clive.

His initial response was one I was familiar with. He pointed out that people were calling into his shop on a regular basis, trying to sell him goods. He had people calling in to him nearly every day, but the promised goods usually failed to meet with his high standards, or to the price promised.

I assured him that I had considerable experience in supplying dealer customers, including overseas trade. We kept our overheads low and thus could guarantee a genuine wholesale price. Clive went on to explain that he already had a regular supplier, but I could see that he was mellowing. Eventually Clive said, 'Ok, bring me a load to look at on your next trip to see your dad'. I agreed, and rang him near the time to finalise arrangements.

The first delivery did not disappoint. We were given a cheque, and a promise to keep in touch.

My technique was always to make a list of the load with the asking price for each item, and hand it to the customer on arrival before starting to unload. This meant that there would be no chance of increasing the price if the prospective purchaser showed enthusiasm for any particular item, something which, I had been informed by a few of my trade customers, was common practice.

We continued to deal very successfully with Clive at the Pine Merchant in Cambridge. He usually purchased a full van load of furniture every month. I continued to supply him after dad died, but now we made the return journey in one day.

We later purchased a very large van which enabled us to combine the trip to Cambridge with a delivery to Windsor, and from there on to Eastleigh near Southampton to stock up from Tony for the return trip. A journey of more than 600 miles in one day.

When Clive decided to sell up and retire, he had been taking regular monthly deliveries from us for over ten years. He recommended us to the new owner, Birgit, whom we continued to supply. Birgit renamed the shop "The Orangerie". More about that later.

Meanwhile, since our shop in New Hall Lane was not producing many customers, Cathy successfully applied for a part-time job with the catalogue company Great Universal Stores, or "GUS". Her shifts were mainly in the evenings, so she was able to go straight from our shop to the call centre, which was situated at the other end of New Hall Lane, nearer to the town centre.

The job was taking telephone orders and involved the use of a computer, which at the age of forty-seven was very daunting as she had never touched one before. Watching all the youngsters clicking away at the keyboards as if they were born to it, made her determined to conquer it. Her mindset was 'if they can do it, I can do it'. And she did.

She enjoyed processing the orders and talking to the customers, and was so successful that eventually she was given the job of training the new recruits. Taking this part-time job brought about the unexpected and very welcome bonus of learning how to use a computer, which of course is now invaluable to our business in this day and age.

In addition to all this, Cathy worked two days a week as housekeeper and cleaner for our Parish Priest, Father Brennan, at St Oswald's in Longton. This started as a short-term favour, but she remained with him until he retired. He became a good friend of our family.

Stephen was now living back at home with us, having completed five years at Up Holland, and was studying for his A-levels. To ease the burden on Cathy, it was decided that Stephen would go into the shop on New Hall Lane on Saturdays. This worked fine for us all, as Stephen could study for his A levels in the shop, with only very rare interruptions from customers!

I was greatly surprised when Stephen rang me one Saturday afternoon in great excitement! He informed me that a French dealer had called into the shop, was interested in quite a few items, and wanted me to go into the shop there and then to meet him. It transpired that this French dealer had been dealing regularly, over several years, with David Plumb from Grimsargh near Preston, buying pub signs. He had in fact been on his way there and had detoured into Preston to collect a book which he had ordered from Waterstones, when he passed our shop. Pure chance!

He explained to Stephen that he would return to our shop after picking up his book. I was extremely busy preparing orders for my existing customers, and was very reluctant to leave what I was doing on the basis that this was most likely just another waste of time.

However, Stephen was adamant that this was a genuine buyer who was extremely interested, and would definitely buy some of our stock. He began to get quite agitated with my reluctance to listen to him. So I relented.

When I arrived at the shop, the French gentleman and his wife had already returned, and were waiting with great enthusiasm for my arrival. He introduced himself and his wife as Fred and Sylvie Sygroves, from Auxerre - some 30 miles from Paris. He was every bit as charming and pleasant and eager as Stephen had said.

He indicated which items he was interested in, and explained that he was an experienced dealer in English furniture and had been, for some years, trading with dealers in Leek, Staffordshire. He was very complimentary about the quality and finish of our stock. He was also honest enough to say that our prices were considerably less than what he had been paying in Leek.

I was a reluctant seller that day. We already had many trade customers, and I was not a fan of the usual method of payment by French dealers, which was to send payment once the goods had reached their destinations in France. I had witnessed the difficulties that some other dealers had experienced when payment was delayed, or even failed to materialise.

And I told Fred exactly that.

He was extremely sympathetic to my point of view. He offered to send an English cheque to David Plumb if I would be willing to deliver the items to Grimsargh and collect the cheque directly from Plumbs. We agreed.

He selected seven items from the stock in the shop that day, with the promise that he would buy many more in the future. And he did.

We went on to deal with Fred for several years. His business name was quite unique. "Le Taxi Mauve". He became a very valued and pleasant customer to deal with. Occasionally, in subsequent years, he asked me to collect his purchases from other dealers and establishments around the country, so that everything was in one place (our premises) to facilitate easy collection by his French transport company. Unlike his American counterparts who expected me to do this for nothing, Fred was willing, indeed insistent, on paying me generously for this service.

A few years into our successful dealings with Fred, he asked if I could also collect and polish items of reproduction pine furniture, which he purchased from Coach House, and we did. Shortly after this, Fred asked if I would do some similar work (polishing the reproduction pine) for a French dealer friend of his. There was a clear understanding that I would not sell any antique items to his friend - he requested that we reserve the antique furniture for himself!!! The arrangement with this new French contact was that we would collect the reproduction furniture, finish and wax it, and he would personally come to England and collect it directly from us.

And so we met Peter Spence!

Peter was equally as pleasant and charming and honest as Fred, and paid on collection with an English cheque, and he was never any problem. He strictly adhered to his (and our) side of the agreement with Fred that we would not sell him any of the antique pine.

Eventually, with changing times and fashions in antique furniture, both of these dealers faded away. As this chapter says, times they were a-changing.

Before completing his final orders with us, Peter brought over his wife to meet us and took us out for a meal to thank us for all we had done. Peter was very interesting, as well as a charming and kind man. He had previously worked as a reporter, which had taken him to many parts of the world, including Hong Kong. He had moved to France at the age of five and lived there ever since. He was now in his sixties and spoke perfect English.

Fred's English was very good but more halting and hesitant, which made our conversations very "interesting" on both parts. Both dealers were frequent visitors to our home.

Peter lived in a beautiful and very large chateau in Brittany, which they had spent many years renovating, and now they, together with his five grown up children, ran it as a B&B. During his many visits to us he showed us photographs of the chateau, which was truly stunning, and some of the outbuildings which he was converting to holiday lets.

Peter repeatedly invited us over to stay with them. He emphasised that this would be on the understanding that we would be their guests, and that we would be no trouble to them as they were used to visitors. However, being the reluctant overseas traveller that I am, we never took him up on his kind offers.

Our earliest experiences of sending furniture overseas, again to France, had been whilst still at our shop in Fox Street Preston. We had several regular customers at this little shop, and one of these was Krishner, a civil engineer who worked for Lancashire County Council. He was from Mauritius and his wife hailed from France. They lived at Lytham, but also had a home in France at Montelimar (home of the famous nougat). They had decided to set up an antique shop there, and bought quite a few items from us on a regular basis.

At the start, we helped him with loading his van etc. Later, when he began to buy larger quantities, we arranged shipping through Edmondsons, the international removal company. They had two young boys, and as we also had young children they spent some time with us at Christmas, and we were visitors to their home in Lytham. We were invited to visit their home in France, and they gave us the option of either going whilst they themselves were holidaying there, or going on our own and having their house to ourselves. But we never did take them up on their very generous offer.

Once we had originally become established in New Hall Lane, we had gained several French customers. The biggest single order we ever received from a French dealer was from Phillip Gribinski from Paris, who ordered 80 chests of drawers in one transaction.

Over the years, we have traded with many dealers from overseas - many from the United States. The majority were appreciative of a good deal and our level of service, much of which was a goodwill gesture on our part with the aim of building up regular repeat business.

One such dealer, Jeff Deprez, who traded as Lonesome Pine in San Francisco, became interested in English antiques after he met and married an English girl - an air stewardess based in Manchester. His main occupation was selling pipe work and ancillary components to the oil and gas industry in America. The antique business was a side line, and he relied heavily on my knowledge and input on the ground over here in England. He became a very good customer and would send money in advance with his order.

We packed his orders in twenty-foot containers in our yard ready for shipping. Haydn Latham dealt with all the shipping documents, custom requirements, and transport to the ports. When Jeff expanded and required larger containers, we introduced him to West Lancs Exports at Burscough. When he came over on his buying trips, we would ensure that we had a plentiful supply of his favourite biscuits - digestives, and occasionally he would stay with us overnight, and of course he had his evening meal with us. On these visits I would take him all around the area to call on other dealers, free of charge as part of my service.

One day, Jeff happened to mention that he had purchased, "back in the States", a fabulous antique pine wardrobe of English origin, which unfortunately had some part of the cornice missing, and he was disappointed that he could not find anyone in the states to repair it. I told him that my son Kevin would be able to repair and restore it. He was extremely sceptical, and reiterated that he had been unable to find anyone in America to do it. I simply replied that Kevin had done similar work very successfully.

Imagine our surprise when, on Jeff's next visit to us, he produced the cornice of that wardrobe. He had brought it over with him on the plane. Kevin did a superb job of the restoration, and with Kevin's skilful repair and our careful staining and waxing, the replaced part was indistinguishable from the original. The cornice was returned to Jeff in his next container load of furniture.

After two or three years, Jeff blotted his copy book. Big Time!

I had charged him the princely sum of £60 to travel, at his request, to Leek in Staffordshire, to collect a very large wardrobe, bring it back, re-strip and re-polish it (again at Jeff's request, as in his opinion it was not fit for sale in the condition it was in) and then deliver it to Burscough to be shipped. And all this within a timescale of 48 hours.

He wanted the £60 to be refunded because he considered that it was too much. I was staggered beyond belief. So, while sitting at my table, eating my biscuits, and using my phone, he reluctantly settled on £30, adding 'I don't think that either of us are going to be happy about this.' He was right.

I concluded our business amicably enough, but I resolved there and then that he would not be sitting at my table again. In short, he was sacked.

Prior to dealing with Jeff, we had been doing business with a group of three friends who were from Maine, USA – you may remember that we met them at Park Hall Antiques Fair. Although they were not big buyers, they were regular buyers and very friendly. We got on well with them and they often had a meal with us when they came to buy. They explained to us how they had to time the arrival of the containers into Maine before the winter weather hit. They needed to get it unloaded, and as much as possible sold, before the "Big Freeze".

Their shipper was based in Market Harborough, and eventually they decided to concentrate their buying activities in the south of England - and so we lost touch. However, one of this group, Paul, went on the Appalachian Trail; this was a 2,000-mile hike across America, taking many months. We were very interested in this, and he regularly sent us postcards from several places on route.

During our business with Jeff, we were simultaneously trading with Maria's Antiques, from California. Maria, and her daughter Rita, came twice a year to buy. We had dealt with Maria from our first shop on New Hall Lane, and subsequently resurrected contact with her via the antiques fair at Park Hall.

Maria was an excellent buyer, usually spending between £6,000 and £8,000 each time, but she would leave annoying little instructions such as "change handles" and other little tweaks. I always felt that she did not quite trust us to carry out her instructions, despite our years of dealing with her, but of course we always did. She would leave our cheque with Haydn, her shipper, with instructions that he must check that we had carried out all her requests before handing over the cheque to us.

Despite this, all went well for a number of years, until one particular visit when Rita (the daughter) was in an absolutely foul mood. She found fault with everything, and angrily demanded to know why I had increased my prices so much.

I kept my cool, and pointed out that if she checked her paperwork from previous visits, she would see that the price range of my goods had not changed in the previous five years. I remember that it was a Sunday, quite late in the evening when they arrived, and she was probably tired and jet lagged - but there was no getting away from, or excusing, the fact that she was extremely rude to me.

My furniture was the same price as before, and was of the same high quality as always. Maria purchased a large quantity that evening, around £6,000 worth of goods. However, during the whole of these proceedings, over the several hours whilst Maria was choosing her items, Rita still kept muttering that she could not understand why my prices had increased so much.

On delivering their purchases to Haydn for shipping, I confided in him what Rita had said, and how rude she had been. He showed me their shipping manifest, which clearly showed what they had bought elsewhere, and the prices they had paid. The cheapest chest of drawers (for example) which she had purchased elsewhere was £50 dearer than any that she had bought from me.

I was incredibly angry at the way Rita had treated me, which was clearly unwarranted, and Rita must have been aware of this. As I drove back home, I resolved that we would part company.

The following spring, on their next prearranged visit, I made sure that all my available stock was already sold. Fortunately, I had a wide range of customers at this time, and I simply did not reserve any for Maria and Rita as I normally would have done. Maria was clearly disappointed and protested, asking why I had not kept some stock for her as I knew she was coming. I explained that Rita had made it very clear that she had considered that my prices were too high for her, so I did not expect her to purchase from me this time.

She got the message, and we did not deal again.

Another dealer who we lassoed from the antiques fair at Park Hall was an eccentric who hailed from North Carolina. Mark Crumpler.

Mark was easily recognisable. He always sported a large colonial-type white pith helmet, and a big fat Havana cigar was always in his mouth. He was extremely pleasant to deal with, provided that you laughed at his jokes, despite having heard them time and time again. We have a very interesting and amusing story regarding Mark.

One day, after he had purchased his dozen or so lots from me, he asked me to go outside and wait for him. His words were 'Please can you just go outside and wait for a few moments, and don't look round.'

Mystified, I did as he asked.

He paid for his items, told his usual jokes, but before he left, he decided that he should explain. Taking me back into the building, he lifted the lid of a bedding chest that he had purchased and pulled open one of the little candle drawers inside. Previously empty, this now contained what appeared to be a roll of cloth.

He retrieved this, unwrapped it, and revealed a colt revolver.

'You have not seen this', he said.
He rewrapped it, placed it back in the drawer, closed the lid again, and then explained.
'I always carry this gun with me at home. I had forgotten I had it on me when I left for my trip over.'

He had travelled through security and customs in both America and the UK, and it had not been discovered. Now he had a dilemma!!!!

If he was caught with it in the UK, it might cause a diplomatic incident. If it was discovered on his person as he attempted to board a plane for his return journey, he would certainly be arrested. He decided that he would get it shipped back in the container with his purchases.

He stressed to me that no one else was aware of this, except for me and Cathy. He later told me that it had arrived back home safely with no mishaps, and was back where it belonged.

His last visit to us saw him flying into a rage because there was a particularly nice piece of furniture which I had already sold to another customer. He believed that I should have kept it for him. His lady friend who accompanied him on that occasion managed to calm him down, and he went on to purchase his usual number of items.

Although that was the last visit to us directly, we did continue to do business with Mark for many more years, but on a more casual basis from our stands at Antique Fairs such as Newark and Swinderby. He was always a colourful character, not easily forgotten.

Chapter 22
Final Farewell to 266 New Hall Lane.

The shop we had purchased at 266 New Hall Lane continued to be a drag and a source of constant regret. I had made no secret of the fact that I had gone against my gut feeling when we bought it, but with the pressure to operate the "rollover" for Capital Gains Tax, and the subsequent stress of dealing with the Inland Revenue, I had finally conceded and gone ahead, but almost immediately regretted it.

When even Cathy became disillusioned at the lack of customers and took the part-time job at GUS, its fate was sealed; it had to go.

At first, we placed it in the hands of a local estate agent on New Hall Lane, just a few doors down, thinking that it would attract local interest. The agent valued it at only £25,000 which was £7,000 less than we had paid for it, not including the £5,000 which had been spent to seal the roof and guttering, and other necessary repairs.

Even at that price there was little interest.

In desperation I offered it to the neighbour next door, an Indian gentleman who operated a business doing television and electronics repairs. He and his wife and their two teenage daughters lived above their shop, and desperately needed more space. Even though I offered him a special price of £24,000, he felt unable to afford it. They were a nice family and we got on well. I think he appreciated the offer but declined, so after several months we were back to square one.

At this point our old friend and ex-partner in the milk business, John Beesley, heard about the dilemma and came up with a plan. He and his wife Margaret still had their milk round but were planning to sell it, as we had.

John's suggestion was that they would buy a half-share based on the estate agent's estimate of £25,000, so £12,500, and then he and I would convert the property from a shop into two flats, proposing that we spent two days a week doing the work ourselves and only bringing in tradesmen to do electrical and gas work - therefore keeping the costs to a minimum.

John was very skilled in many areas of DIY, having completed an extension on his own home and lots of work at Hill View for us. It seemed a good solution, so we accepted his offer and set about the legal formalities of the purchase, and then sought planning approval for a change of use from commercial premises to residential.

The application for change of use met with some resistance, since the planning department at Preston Council insisted that it was a designated commercial area, and they suggested we retain a shop on the ground floor with a single flat above. Exasperated, and sick of this white elephant, I angrily told the planning officer that since we had found the shop to be non-viable, if we could not convert it to residential use then we would have no alternative but to board it up and leave it empty. They finally relented, and with planning permission granted for change of use to two flats, John and I were able to start the intense work of conversion.

There was still a demand for student accommodation in Preston at that time, so with some urgency we pressed on with the aim of getting the flats on the market in time for the new academic year in September. With the pressure to hit this target it became necessary to put in an extra day per week, which I found difficult due to being busy with the antique pine and all the associated work of sanding, waxing, and repairing it.

I was fortunate to be able to get lots of part time help from some of Kevin's friends, notably Peter Kelly - who came three times a week including Saturdays, and one or two others who helped on an occasional basis. As a result, we managed (just) to keep up with doing what paid the bills (preparing the pine furniture), which in turn enabled an increase in the intensity of activities required to get the property finished.

As completion neared, we placed the letting with an agency, who very quickly found student tenants for each of the two flats at quite a reasonable rent. The first few months went very smoothly, and I was able to concentrate on sourcing, processing, and selling pine furniture, which fortunately was still very much in demand.

Student accommodation by the next academic year was plentiful through the university directly, and the agency failed to find new student tenants. We undertook to advertise the flats ourselves on the open market, and through market research we found it necessary to reduce the rent to below that which had been paid by the students the year before.

We quickly found tenants, and over the next couple of years there was much coming and going. Some were alright, others a pain - always complaining about something. Each time there was a change of tenant, we had the task of cleaning the flats and doing any necessary work before advertising it again.

One particular couple were quite good tenants but when they left, after refunding their deposit, we discovered that they had kept a house rabbit which had frequently made a meal of the stair carpet. They had disguised this by gluing bits back in, so that it was not discovered until we were doing the cleaning.

In the meantime, John and Margaret had sold their milk round, and John had developed a reclusive lifestyle and become difficult to contact. More and more of the work at change-over fell to Cathy and myself.

Cathy was charged with collecting the rent when she finished her shift at GUS, extending her long days even further, and when the last tenant frequently failed to pay - with different excuses every time, what had been a nuisance job became a nightmare. Then the wall dividing the back yard collapsed, and while it was down someone helped themselves to the York stone flags of the backyard! Worth quite a few hundred pounds I was told! It cost £800 to get the wall rebuilt, and more money to put concrete flags down to replace the stolen ones, so that once again the tenants were able to access the backyard.

When the bad payer left, we did not re-let that flat. The remaining tenant in the other flat was a young girl who kept the flat spotless and paid her rent, but constantly complained of being cold - her origins being from sunnier climes. Eventually we managed to track John down, and secured his agreement to market the flats. We had had enough!

We marketed them through an agent in Preston town centre, who although showed great enthusiasm to take it on, still only valued the combined unit at £25,000. Their initial advertising produced some interest, but nothing solid. After several months, an offer of £24,000 was made, to which we reluctantly agreed, and the solicitor was instructed.

The potential buyer, having secured the acceptance of his offer, indicated that he would instruct a surveyor, but then seemed to go to ground and failed to answer the solicitor's letters and calls, and no surveyor appeared. We were in limbo again. Then unexpectedly things began to happen!!

We received a phone call one evening from someone introducing himself as a builder, and expressing a keen interest in the property at 266 New Hall Lane. I was somewhat unsure where he had got our home number from, certainly not the agent, but possibly from the remaining tenant.

He certainly seemed genuine and asked if the property was still available. On hearing of the situation, he promised to ring again the next night, and did so. His opening sentence was that he definitely wanted to buy it.

I referred him to the agent, and the next day I contacted our solicitor and told her to write to the original potential purchaser and give him an ultimatum. She did so, giving him two weeks to contact us or we would sell elsewhere.

The builder rang again the next evening, and confessed that he was really acting as an intermediary on behalf of the owner of the shop adjoining us (on the other side, not the TV repair man). He had asked the builder to contact me on his behalf, believing that because he was Asian, I would not deal with him. I found the suggestion absurd and ridiculous, and assured the builder that this was not the case at all. He passed on this message to his client and, sure enough, the gentleman concerned rang me the following evening.

He introduced himself and explained his enthusiasm to buy since he owned the shop next door, and immediately offered the full asking price. I endeavoured to explain the legal procedure we were obliged to follow, and that the other potential buyer still had a week in which to respond, and until then we could not accept his kind offer.

Two days later he upped his offer by another £2,000 but I was forced to give him the same response, and referred him to our solicitor who gave him a detailed explanation. The following day our agent called to say that he had a gentleman in the office anxious to buy our property - with literally a bag full of cash!

Of course, we were unable to accept it, but assured him that as soon as the legal notice expired, we would be pleased to accept. The phantom buyer with the original offer never did respond, so when the two-week period expired our solicitor immediately contacted our impatient neighbour, by which time his offer was up to £28,000, some £3,000 more than the original market price.

To our immense relief the sale went through relatively unimpeded, the only hiccup being persuading John to go to the solicitor's office to sign the papers. Cathy managed to find him, persuade him, take him to the solicitors office at Winckley Square, and then accompanied him inside to make sure that he signed the document.

Despite getting a better price than we had expected, we had still lost money over the original purchase price. At least this time there was no capital gains tax to deal with. Selling what I had regarded as a huge millstone around my neck was a relief, and now I could concentrate on what I loved best: antique dealing.

Chapter 23
Re-discovering the antique fairs.

Having moved on from the shop, the last two or three years of the 1990's saw us re-examining the role of the antique fairs in our business.

As far the antique *centres* went, there were several operating in the Preston area. Bygone Times had been our most successful and we had been there for over eight years, but we had also spent time in Preston Antique Centre (The Mill), GB Antiques at Lancaster, and Heskin Hall. Alongside this we had our many trade customers, but as with most things in life the antique business does not stand still, and we realised that we had to widen our horizons.

Over the years we had previously attended various fairs such as Park Hall, The Floral Hall in Southport, The Winter Gardens Blackpool, Cheltenham Racecourse, Newbury Racecourse, Haydock Racecourse, Stoneleigh in Warwickshire, Trentham Gardens in Staffordshire, and Birmingham Rag Market in the Bullring.

I attended the Birmingham Rag Market on many occasions, once taking my mother-in-law when she was visiting, which she hugely enjoyed even though we had to be up and away from Leyland before 4am.

The really big one of course was Newark, which despite everyone in the trade talking about, I had never been until that first visit with Keith which I referred to earlier. I visited Newark several times after Keith's death with Kevin when he was working with me, but also on various occasions with Cathy, Alison or Maggie, and in later years, as soon as he was old enough, our grandson Leigh.

I decided to revisit Newark as a stallholder, as also to try Swinderby (which had become as big and as internationally recognised as Newark).

Most of the fairs at which we took stands were outside pitches, except for Stoneleigh where we took a stand within a drive-in building. Being under cover had the distinct advantage that it was possible to display polished furniture, such as pine, without the risk of damage by the elements.

Stoneleigh was held at the Royal Showground, and I usually attended this one alone. I enjoyed considerable success with the polished pine, selling most of my stock each time to the same two or three dealers. One of these was Richard - trading as Pine and Things at Shipston on Stour, which was only half an hour's drive from the fair. Most of these fairs only met with mediocre success, but Stoneleigh had been different and had been profitable.

Kevin had, by this time, developed his own very successful bespoke furniture business, and was no longer working full time with me.

Cathy and I had taken a stall at the Swinderby Fair, where we stood on Thursdays and Fridays. We went to Park Hall fair on Sundays to buy stock, and then to Newark on Monday and Tuesday to sell. A very intensive few days.

Newark and Swinderby fairs were by now very busy, and to secure a regular spot dealers needed to commit to all the fairs - six a year. Prime busy pitches were jealously guarded, and booking a "casual" meant potluck on where you would be sited in the vast showroom grounds. Cathy's role, as usual, was to man the stall 90% of the time, using her charm to sell, whilst I roamed the fair searching for goods to buy and chatting to contacts and fellow stallholders.

At Newark, one such stallholder was a dealer from Preston Antique Centre who had an outdoor pitch such as ours - but in a prime location. We stayed for both days of the fair, sleeping in our van, but he only stood for the first day, so he kindly offered us the opportunity to move on to his pitch in this prime location for the second day of trading. This proved beyond any doubt that position was everything, as we frequently sold more than double on the second day compared with the first day.

This prime spot of his was quite close to an area known as the "shopping arcades" which were long and low marquee structures with individual interior divisions, creating undercover shops. The proximity of these arcades enabled us to examine the quality and price of the goods on offer there, and it quickly became apparent that this was a higher-class area with more expensive goods, attracting a more discerning type of customer.

The rent for these units was more than double what we were paying for an outside pitch, but it was obvious that you could display better quality, higher priced goods. Furthermore, a huge advantage of the shopping arcades for us was that there was space to put a caravan at the rear of the stall.

The prospect of sleeping in the comfort of our caravan rather than the van was very appealing, so we made the decision to apply for one of these shopping arcades. We were fortunate enough to be offered a unit for the very next fair.

We took a varied selection of stock to this next fair - our usual pine furniture, together with hardwood items such as oak and mahogany, a considerable variety of pictures (watercolours, oils, etc. for which I had constructed a pegboard display stand), plus Cathy's favourite – ceramics, as well as antique biscuit barrels, of which she had a very large selection.

Stall holders were permitted access on the afternoon before the fair opened, to allow time to set out the stall and park the caravan, which was necessary because trading started at 5.30am on selling days. Our first day there did not disappoint. We sold steadily from the opening - a wide variety of items including many of the pictures, which was very encouraging.

The young man I had met at Stoneleigh (Richard, from Pine and Things) was there at Newark too, and he bought a considerable amount of the pine. We met a lovely couple, Caroline and her partner Paul, who also bought some of the pine, with the added bonus that they asked if we had more stock available if they came to Preston - thus future contact was assured.

Caroline and Paul dealt with us for several years until Caroline's premature death at the age of 39. This was extremely sad. They had been up to see us just a few days before, and it was a total shock. Her funeral, which was in Oxfordshire, took place while Cathy was over in Ireland, but I felt I had to pay my respects to this lovely young lady, and attended the funeral. We have remained in touch with Paul to this day.

Our first experience of the arcades was so successful that we booked the next and subsequent fairs without hesitation. We attended each of the Newark fairs, six a year, until 2003. The atmosphere was very friendly, and one of our near neighbours in the shopping marquee was Martin, with whom I had shared the large pitch in the City Road Antique centre in Chester. Martin was on hand to help me unload, and I returned the favour.

These years standing as a regular at the Newark fair brought us several regular customers.

Caroline, of course, whom I have already mentioned.

Another was Ben Eccleston from Long Martin in Cumbria, to whom I sold a lot of pine "in the paint" and, as he was an importer of European Pine, I frequently bought furniture from him when I delivered what he had purchased from us to his premises in Cumbria.

Another important contact made at Newark Fair was Simon Byrne of Eastburn Pine in West Yorkshire. Once again, we went on to do business with Simon for a considerable number of years, selling him pine "in the paint". This also led to him being introduced to Kevin, who by now was making bespoke kitchens and furniture. Simon was able to utilise Kevin's skills, workshop and manpower, as an overflow when Simon himself was busy to the point that his own facilities could not manage the workload. This working arrangement continues to this day.

The success at Newark Fair encouraged me to stand at another fair run by the same organiser (ICAF), which was held at the West of England Showground, Shepton Mallet. These fairs were also a two-day event (but on a Saturday and Sunday) with setting up of stands from Friday midday.

Unfortunately, on the day we were due to go to this fair, our youngest son Stephen was taken very ill. Cathy stayed with Stephen, and I went to the fair accompanied by our daughter Maggie. We managed to leave our home in Longton at around noon that day, and began what was to become a very long and arduous journey. The weather was hot, and I had not factored into the equation the huge amount of weekend holiday traffic heading for the west country.

We spent a considerable time in traffic on the M5, and furthermore I had not fully realised just how far we had to go. We did not reach the showground until 8pm, by which time we were both tired and hungry. On arrival at the showground gates, we were somewhat mystified to find them shut, preventing entry.

After what seemed an age, a security man ambled up to the inside of the gates. He knew nothing in detail about the antique fair as he was employed by the showground owners. He did know that there was an antique fair on the site, but told us that the organisers had left for the night. I showed him my booking ticket and he very reluctantly opened the gate and let me in, but he had no knowledge of the layout of the fair and suggested that I ask someone when I reached the area where the fair was arranged.

Enquiries were made with other stall holders who were roaming around, and they directed us to the area where the shopping arcades were situated. Once we located the general area, it did not take long to find our allocated pitch - since most were already occupied. In fact, our pitch and the one adjacent were the only empty spaces.

We quickly parked the caravan. By now, both of us were completely exhausted, and while Maggie made us some food, I unloaded as much of the van as I could, and began to set up the stall. It had been an exhausting journey, and an extremely long day.

Refreshed, and somewhat relieved, we retired for the night and set the alarm for any early start so that we could finish unloading and complete the stall set-up, ready for customers. The next morning, as quickly as I could, I set out a wide variety of stock similar to that which normally sold so well at Newark. Maggie made what was to be the first of many bacon butties, which she produced all day long.

Shortly before the fair was due to open, a van appeared and backed into the empty space next to me. Out hopped Jon Swires, a dealer I knew from Preston Antique Centre, fresh as a daisy. He had spent the night at a nearby Travelodge! He was quite unperturbed that he was the last to arrive.

I was pleased to see a friendly face, and he was just in time to help me unload a very heavy bedroom suite. I was able to return the favour and helped him to unload his furniture just as the first visitors to the fair began to arrive.

Sales were slow. Not just for me, but for Jon also.

On the positive side, it was a beautiful day - but very hot. Jon was really chuffed to be offered a steady supply of drinks, together with our bacon butties, all day long. The fair closed at 5pm with poor results and very few sales.

Jon set off back to his travel lodge for the night, and Maggie and I went into Shepton Mallet to explore, and to stock up our supplies of bacon and treats. The second day's trading was no better than the first, and we set about packing up our unsold items early in the afternoon. I was grateful for Jon's help to load the heavy bedroom suite back into the van!

With sales so slow I had not been scouting around the fair looking for stock to buy, as I normally would. But a quick mid-afternoon sortie on the Sunday brought me face to face with Martin, my near neighbour at the Newark Fair, and former fellow dealer at City Road Antique Centre in Chester. As time went on, I was to meet Martin at every large fair I ever visited, including the Antiques for Everyone Fair at the NEC in Birmingham.

When the fair closed, we finished loading up, hitched up the caravan, joined the long queue of vehicles exiting the showground, and readied ourselves for the very long journey home. I already knew by then that we would not be repeating our visit to this fair!

To add to the frustrations of the weekend, as we left the showground, I realised that my phone was no longer working. Having left it on the dashboard in the van for a short time while we finished loading, it had become overheated in the extremely hot sunshine and was no longer functioning. It was so hot I could not even hold it. When we hit the open road, and as soon she was able to handle it, Maggie held the phone out of the window and after about thirty minutes of cooling it down, to my great relief it came back to life.

It was a tedious journey, but we got home safely. With less traffic on the road, the return trip only took about six hours. It was fortunate that Cathy had decided not to come with me on that occasion as Stephen was indeed very ill, hospitalised, and remained in hospital for several weeks.

The experience at Shepton Mallet made it an easy decision not to attend that fair again, but Newark continued to prove its worth. Richard (Pine and Things) had become a regular customer, along with several others.

In 1999, our daughter Alison commenced her studies at Oxford University. When Richard heard that we would be taking her to Oxford, he suggested that we call at his premises on route with a few items of stripped pine, to keep him "topped up" and contribute towards our costs in travelling down. This proved so successful that it quickly became a regular monthly delivery, which continued for well over ten years until he emigrated to the USA.

In October 2000, whilst standing at our regular spot at the Newark Fair, I became aware of, and bothered by, an uncomfortable sensation which felt like spots in my right eye. I mentioned this to Martin when he was, as usual, assisting me in loading my many purchases. Without hesitation, he advised me to get it looked at asap, adding the comment 'you can't be too careful with your eyes Dave.'

The next day I contacted my GP for an appointment. He examined me briefly and told me that I should take my problem to an optician immediately, and declined to comment on what could be the cause. I attended Specsavers two days later for an afternoon appointment - at 2.30pm on October 20th, which happened to be Maggie's 18th birthday.

After conducting the usual eye test and field of vision test, the optician informed me that I had to go straight to Preston hospital. He arranged it, declined to speculate on what could be the problem, but stressed that I had to go immediately. More than a little alarmed, Cathy drove me to the hospital. We were very conscious of the fact that it was Maggie's 18th, and a celebration meal was booked for the entire family that evening.

When we reached the eye clinic at Preston Hospital we were seen immediately. Throughout the afternoon I was subjected to various tests, including the field vision. At 5pm, anxious about the evening meal, I asked how much longer I would be required to stay and was informed at least another two hours. Hearing this news, we rang home and arranged that they should all go ahead to the meal, and we would meet up with them later.

I was finally seen by yet another doctor at around 7.30pm, who advised that they had not reached a conclusion as to the problem, but I was to attend the eye clinic twice a week for the next few weeks.

We finally arrived at the meal about 8.30pm.

Over the coming weeks I attended the eye clinic twice weekly, and was subjected to a whole series of tests culminating in the obligatory field of vision test, before then being seen by a series of different optical specialists. During all this time, the vision in my right eye had changed from spots to a sense of blurring.

On one memorable occasion, I was sent for an ultrasound scan on my neck at Preston Maternity Hospital. On arrival, I was sent into a separate room to change, and when I joined the very heavily pregnant ladies in the waiting room, I got some very strange looks!

It was approximately four weeks into these intensive examinations when I was finally seen by the main consultant, who informed me that the condition I had was known as Anterior Ischemic Optic Neuropathy - a very rare condition not seen by many opticians throughout their career, and hence the intensity of the tests before a diagnosis could be made.

He went on to explain that the cause was a minute blood clot in the capillaries supplying the optic nerve. It was sudden, gave no warning, and was irreversible. The nerves supplying that part of the eye were dead and there was no treatment. The bottom half of my right eye was now blind. He advised that I would still be able to legally drive because I still had good vision in one eye, but I should allow a few months before driving long distances, or driving at night, in order to allow the other eye to adjust.

My final question was to enquire about the likelihood of the left eye going the same way. He replied somewhat philosophically that there was no certainty, but it was far more likely to happen to me a second time than to ever happen to the person standing next to me in a bus queue! I further asked if working in a dusty environment such as sanding furniture could be a contributing factor, and he replied 'No'.

We drove home knowing that we had to make some adjustments to our work schedule over at least the next few months. Our next delivery to Richard at Pine and Things was imminent, so Richard willingly drove up to Lancashire to collect his order.

Before all this happened, we had loosely planned that when I reached retirement age at sixty-five, we would take some weekends away to our old haunts in Cambridge, having seen enticing advertisements in the Antiques Gazette for Willingham auction and also Dyson and Sons auction at Clare.

We had speculated that we could attend these auctions, stay overnight, and hopefully buy enough unusual items (which they seemed to have an abundance of there) to finance a weekend away every month.

Clare is a delightful small market town where I had delivered milk in my younger years - I knew the town well. It is situated in an idyllic part of the world and is just a few miles from where we had lived when we first set up home in Linton, allowing us the opportunity to revisit our old haunts.

After the eyesight diagnosis, we spent the winter months musing over the fact that if my eyesight deteriorated further before I reached retirement age, we would be unable to enact those plans.

It was decided. In the spring of the next year, 2001, we would have a trial run.

Chapter 24
Journey back to Home Turf.

The auction at Willingham was about ten miles north of Cambridge, also in a district that I was familiar with from my earlier milk delivery days with the Co-Op dairy. These auctions were held every four weeks, and those at Dyson and Sons at Clare in Suffolk were held every three weeks.

This meant that periodically both auctions fell on the same Saturday. We decided that it would be best to choose a trial run by going when both sales coincided, so that we could gauge how cost effective and productive it would be.

A prior telephone call to the Willingham saleroom had given me quite a considerable amount of confidence, as it was confirmed (as the advertisements had suggested) that they regularly had a good selection of antique pine in the sales, and the prices that I was given as a guide were very encouraging. I was informed that they operated two sales running simultaneously, each starting at 10am. It was also confirmed that we could collect our purchases and leave without having to wait until the end of the sale, which was not possible in some salerooms. It was very clear that we would be welcomed as a new client.

I knew the distance from Cambridge to Clare was about thirty-five miles, so we made plans to leave early on the Friday morning in order to view the Willingham sale around lunchtime, and then travel on to Clare.

So it was that we set off on our first weekend buying trip on the morning of Friday 30th March 2001, having pre-booked a hotel at Cambridge for our overnight stop. All went to plan. We arrived mid-morning at the Willingham saleroom, briefly viewed the sale, and registered ourselves as buyers. A more detailed examination of the goods on offer revealed many potential buys, which was a pleasing start; we just had to hope that we could secure some of them.

We then travelled on to Clare and had a picnic lunch in Clare Country Park, which had been the old Clare railway station, now closed - one of many victims of Dr Beeching and his notorious axing of the railways in the 1960's. The last time I had been there was some thirty years prior, while delivering milk for the Co-Op. The station had only just closed back then, and I had made it a regular breakfast stop to sit there and have a coffee. This had been a beautiful country station, and when I first started to make it a breakfast stop, it had only been closed for a matter of weeks. It was utterly deserted, with the platform tracks and station buildings totally intact - but eerily quiet.

In the interim years the entire station and station yard, and the surrounding woods, had been converted to a county park, with a large pay and display car park which was a very convenient place to leave our van, as the saleroom was just a few minutes walk away.

The saleroom itself was very small but on two levels. It was incredibly well set out with the lots for sale packing every available space, including a small outside yard where some of the pine was displayed.

We were met at a small front desk by (as we later discovered) the owner's wife. Once registered, we tried to buy a catalogue which was happily handed over, but payment refused. As welcome new customers, payment for the catalogue was considered unnecessary. Once again there were several items of interest, but since we could not attend both sales at the same time, we decided to leave absentee bids with the auctioneer at Clare, and attend the Willingham sale in person, as there was a much larger array of items of interest there.

We returned to Cambridge and checked in to our hotel with a feeling that our trip was all looking very promising. The hotel was situated on Cambridge services and was connected to various shops and food outlets, where we discovered a restaurant with an extremely good deal. This was an "eat all you want" self-service establishment where, for just £5 a head, you could help yourself to hot and cold food. A huge selection was on offer, and you returned to replenish your plates and try any (or all) of the tempting and delicious dishes as often as you wanted. We were in heaven! Happy days.

The Saturday morning saw us arrive at Willingham Auctions with great anticipation. There was a lot to tempt us, and we were hopeful of buying quite a few items. The first part of the sale was conducted in an open-fronted barn structure and consisted of many items for restoration including the painted Victorian pine, so we did not have to wait very long for our first lots to come up for sale.

This first part of the sale was conducted by the young man we had spoken to the day before, when we registered - Will Axon. In later years, Will went on to work for several other well-known salerooms, and was often to be seen on TV programs such as Bargain Hunt and Flog It.

We secured quite a few items early in the sale, and later, two extremely large antique pine tables - something that Richard from Pine and Things had been urgently seeking. In total we spent around £2,500.

In the many years of attending Warren and Wignalls and other salerooms, I had never been able to acquire so much stock at one sale. Not only was there much on offer, but there was unusual and rare stock for us, items that we did normally come across in salerooms in the North.

On this first occasion, having purchased a large amount of furniture and being aware that we had yet to go to Clare, we did not attend the remainder of the sale, nor view the second sale which was running concurrently in the room next door. Instead, we started the mammoth task of loading our purchases onto the van.

In those days we had a high-roof transit with a full-length roof rack, and we were grateful for the offer of assistance from the porter who, in his day job, was a lorry driver - so packing was second nature to him.

The furniture was piled up high on the roof rack. The porter climbed up onto the van roof where his expertise in packing, stacking, and expertly securing all the items was a godsend.

Although it was only March 31st, it was an exceedingly hot day. Loading up had taken well over an hour, and many cool drinks were required during this "operation roof-rack". These were purchased from the on-site cafe which served an excellent range of home baked cakes and my favourite - overfilled and very tasty bacon butties.

By the time we finished, the inside of the van was crammed full, as was the roof rack. There was just a small amount of space between the legs of the upturned large tables, which were up on the roof rack. At this point we were unaware whether or not we had secured any of the ten lots on which we had left bids at Clare.

After several attempts at ringing the Clare auction room, we were finally advised that we had bought three lots. Feeling reasonably confident that we could accommodate them, we set off on the journey to Clare with some urgency, since, from there, our long journey home included a slight detour to deliver several boxes of Victorian ceramic tiles to one of our customers. She was a regular buyer from us at Newark Fair, who trusted our judgement and our descriptions, so was happy to buy from us "unseen".

This detour added about twenty miles to our journey of approximately 235 miles, and was, as we were to find out, a pretty drive along country lanes to yet another picturesque village, where our customer had her unique and interesting shop.

The collection of purchases at the Clare saleroom was via an alleyway at the rear - just wide enough to allow access. Our arrival caused quite a stir with the roof rack already stacked high. After paying for our goods, the two saleroom porters began to help us stack the roof rack even higher, at which point Mr Dyson himself came out for a chat.

It would have been obvious to him, even though we did not consider it so ourselves, that we had the potential to become very big customers, even though we had only secured three items at his sale on this occasion.

I scrambled up to secure the items on the roof; by this time there were quite a few onlookers, and whilst I tied ropes and knotted them in (hopefully) the right places, Mr Dyson was asking us a bit more about ourselves - and then anxiously enquired if we would be coming again.

I replied that yes of course we would, but the next time I would make a point of attending his saleroom in person, as we were impressed with the items for sale but were limited on this occasion because of attending the Willingham sale on the same day.

We commenced the long journey ahead of us at about 4pm, with a van that was full to bursting, and a roof rack piled even higher than before. We certainly attracted a few bemused looks from passing motorists.

It was approximately 6.30pm when we reached our customer's shop to deliver her Victorian tiles, but as she lived on the premises this was not a problem. The tiles were bought, paid for, and our customer was delighted with them. We were back on the road within half an hour.

We arrived home safely at about 10.30pm. It had been a tiring but very fruitful and nostalgic first trip back to our old haunts. We knew it was a trip we would repeat - it had certainly been very interesting, and we hoped that it would also prove to be profitable.

The next day I began the task of unloading the van and was not disappointed when I came to examine everything that I had bought. I began to decide who to assign each piece to. The big tables were definitely to be offered to Richard at Pine and Things, as I felt sure that he would welcome them (and that we would both see a good profit). A few weeks later, with the tables polished and gleaming without a lot of effort from me, he did.

The furniture which needed to be stripped was reloaded and taken to Burnley where, with Bernard Buckley's help, we had located a very good and reasonably priced set-up. Alan, the owner, had worked for many years before at Primrose Antiques where I had done much business, and he remembered me. I usually went over to him weekly, taking items that needed stripping and picking up those that were done.

By 2001, the waxing was mostly down to me and Pete Kelly. Pete was Kevin's boyhood friend who originally came to help me out and earn some pocket money when he was a teenager. He remained a steadfast help for the next thirty-six years, becoming a greatly valued friend to all our family. After he started his working life, he continued to help me every Saturday without fail, except for when he went away on his annual holiday. His help has been invaluable to me, assisting me not only with the antique and restoring business and the myriad tasks entailed with that, but also helping with maintaining and repairing the buildings and the land etc., the list is endless!

We made the decision to repeat the excursion to both salerooms, since we were busy with many good customers and needed the stock. These trips to auctions in the area of my birth and youth were to be fruitful and extremely enjoyable. We were welcomed and treated well by both Colin, the owner at Willingham, and George Dyson, the owner at Clare. It was nice to enjoy an overnight away, and occasionally we stayed for two nights and made a weekend of it. On the Sundays we would go to Mass at English Martyrs Church in Cambridge, and then enjoy a walk around this beautiful city before setting off home.

Several months after we began making regular trips to Willingham, Colin took over Saffron Walden Auctions - holding monthly sales there. It was another opportunity for us to visit old haunts again.

We loved Saffron Walden, and it brought back fond memories. We had visited it often when our children were small, attended mass there, and taken the kids on picnics and walks. It was only five miles from our house when we had lived in Linton. It is a charming "Olde World" small market town, picture postcard perfect, with an abundance of thatched roof cottages and interesting shops.

During my early attempts at being an antique dealer I had, occasionally, taken a stall on Saffron Walden open market in the town centre on Saturdays. I remember the last time that I had stood there. It was just before Christmas, setting up at 7am was by lamp light, and it had started to snow heavily.

Despite the weather, I made a few sales. One very memorable one was to Bernard Miles, actor and comedian, who was well known for his broad Suffolk accent. He bought a pair of watercolours from me. Shortly after that, with the snow falling thick and fast, I decided with some of the other market stall holders to abandon the day, pack up, and get home whilst I still could. The market superintendent didn't come for payment until about 10am, so I got away that day without having to pay!

My last few months prior to moving to Preston in 1974 were spent working for the Cambridge Co-Op delivering milk in and around Saffron Walden. This had been, to me, more like a pleasurable day's outing than hard work.

So, we went to most of the sales in Saffron Walden, and when they clashed with the sale at Clare we would leave bids at Saffron Walden, and attend the auction at Clare - returning via Saffron Walden to collect any purchases made.

These excursions provided good hunting grounds for a variety of stock, mostly pine, but Cathy was also able to indulge her passion for "smalls" and pottery, and thus increase our scope for selling quite a varied range of items at Newark. This was generally a good time, but incredibly busy. However, if you enjoy what you do, it doesn't seem like hard work!

The sales at Clare were a joy to attend and we were always made welcome by Mr and Mrs Dyson. The saleroom was situated right in the centre, adjacent to the parish church, with a sandwich shop almost next door on the other side. Sandwiches were freshly made as you ordered, and were truly delicious. I can remember Cathy and I sitting on the church yard wall in the sunshine eating our lunch, before loading our purchases. Very happy days in a lovely setting.

The auction itself was always conducted with precision by Mr Dyson himself. The space in the room was so limited that the sale was conducted from a box-like rostrum in the corner of the upper part of the saleroom, the floor being of split level. Mr Dyson would access "the box" via a ladder from the lower part. The ladder was then removed by one of his staff members to make floor space for bidders, and there he would remain for the duration of the sale. He would make a few announcements in the five minutes before starting, and then - studying his watch - would commence proceedings at exactly 11am.

No clerk, no internet, just himself!!

He was the fastest and most precise auctioneer I have ever witnessed, and to this day I have seen none better.

He was clear and easy to follow, with just the right amount of humour and banter, and you would certainly not lose concentration while he was in charge. He would be writing down a successful bidder's number while simultaneously introducing the next lot. The sale usually consisted of between 650 and 670 lots, and the sale was usually completed between 2pm and 2.15pm.

There were aways items of interest to us throughout the auction, and so we were usually there for the duration of the sale. When we were attending Clare, or Saffron Walden, we would stay at a Travel Lodge close to Linton, the village where we used to live.

There are two particularly memorable visits to Clare auctions.

On one occasion, when we arrived to view the sale, we came across the largest pine dresser I have ever seen. It was in two parts, with cupboards and drawers to the base and more cupboards above the work surface. Over thirteen feet (yes 13) in length, it was totally as originally constructed, not painted or varnished, and certainly very old. Mr Dyson told me that they had discovered the dresser in the outbuilding of a house which they had been clearing as part of a deceased's estate. I was very keen, and Cathy and I discussed what to do about it for the whole of that evening.

Mr Dyson was well aware of our interest, and I think he knew that he was sure to sell it, much to his relief no doubt, as it took up such a lot of room in his small saleroom. We came on the day of the sale with even more enthusiasm than usual, and proceeded to buy quite an array of goods, but the real excitement was reserved for this dresser, which was the last lot in the sale. I was determined to bid for it but, of course, I had no idea what opposition I would encounter.

Some brisk bidding ensued and finally it was knocked down to me for £670, with Mr Dyson adding the comment at the fall of the hammer, 'I hope you have a big van Sir!!!'

In our usual after-sales chat with Mr Dyson, I informed him that I would have to come back for the dresser, as I had already bought enough to fill the van. He assured me that it was no problem, but requested that we let him know the day and approximate time, so that he could arrange for extra help with the loading.

He was as good as his word.

When we arrived the following Tuesday, doing the journey of 235 miles before 10am, he had assembled a total of five strong men, and with no effort on my part the top section was put on the roof rack, and the base inside the van. We could not shut the van doors because of the length, so they had to be tied to the dresser, making for a rather noisy journey back home.

Mr Dyson had very thoughtfully taken, and printed out, a large picture of the dresser already assembled, so that I could easily show it to potential buyers.

Realising that I would be unable to unload it without help, I called Simon Byrne of Eastburn Pine, one of my regular customers, as we were travelling home. He was very interested and arranged to come over and view it the following morning. He arrived at 8.30am, and the dresser was of course still on (and in) the van. With a bit of clambering onto the roof and with the help of the photograph, he could instantly see its imposing size and uniqueness.

Simon immediately - and with his usual directness - asked just two questions.

'How much is it?' and 'Will you deliver it?'
Of course I would!!

I delivered it that same afternoon. When I arrived, Simon had arranged to borrow a fork-lift truck and the dresser was unloaded. I was on my way home with a cheque tucked away in my pocket within twenty minutes. Simon was delighted with it, and I had almost doubled my money. A nice deal all round.

The other notable excursion to Clare came when the sale in April 2002 fell on the day that Alison was having her 21st birthday party. Mr Dyson was devastated when I rang to tell him that I would not be coming down because, although I was not a great party goer, I could hardly not be there on such an important birthday. He informed me that there was a large amount of pine furniture in the sale, which he was sure was "right up my street". Most of the items would be in the first part of the sale, and he suggested that I could go early, buy the items I was interested in, and then leave - returning at my convenience sometime in the following week to pick up and pay.

I left Hill View in Longton at 4am, attended the sale, and bought lots of furniture. At the fall of the hammer on the last lot of pine in the sale, Mr Dyson paused, and before starting on the next lot he spoke to me directly across the room: 'Thank you Sir, now you get off to your party!'

I attended almost every sale at Willingham and Saffron Walden. If I ever deemed that there were not enough items of interest to justify the trip (which was rare), I would get condition reports and leave bids. I was never disappointed.

I never missed a single sale at Clare with Mr Dyson, and carried on until 2006 when, to my great dismay, Mr Dyson announced his intention to retire.

He spoke to me at some length about his reasons for this: mostly the changing market, but he had also been hit hard by the loss of business from servicemen who had attended his sale from the American Air Base at Lakenheath. They bought furniture, especially oak, to take back home, but following the disaster of 9/11 and the Twin Towers, they were mostly redeployed to Afghanistan. One of these servicemen had gone even further and established a business selling English furniture "back home" and he had been a regular customer at Clare.

Mr Dyson's view was that small salerooms such as his, with low commission rates, could not compete with the changing times. His last sale was rather sad; as a family business they had welcomed us, and we had become - as he told me - a very important part of his business. Clare was such a lovely, pretty place to visit that our trips there did not seem like work, and we would miss it.

We continued with our trips to Willingham and Saffron Walden, always buying a good amount of quality items, so much so that occasionally it was necessary to make a second trip down to collect all our purchases.

One such occasion at Willingham was when there was a large amount of church pews. They were unusual for several reasons: they were in yellow pine (rather than the usual pitch pine) and they also had a box-type base, which made them ideal for domestic use when shortened. They were sold as individual lots and I managed to bid for, and secure, all of them except for one - which went to a very enthusiastic private bidder.

The church pews themselves would have entirely filled the van, so we made the decision to pick up everything else we had bought that day, and then we returned a few days later to pick up the pews.

They required some dismantling! They had been removed from the church complete with all the cast iron central heating pipes still attached to the rear of each one. It took about two hours of hard graft to dismantle them all and load them onto the van. Gail (Colin's wife) very kindly kept us well supplied with coffee and homemade cakes from their onsite coffee shop throughout.

I had already sold the pews to Simon Bryne over the phone, but before delivery to him could be arranged, 9/11 happened and shocked the world. Every single one of Simon's American buyers immediately cancelled their trips over - they refused to fly. However, Simon honoured his agreement with me, bought the pews, and eventually managed to sell them all.

When the Clare saleroom closed, we sought another to replace it. After some research, we decided that "Lacy, Scott and Knight" in Bury St. Edmunds would be ideal for us, especially as this too was held on Saturdays. This turned out to be another very fruitful and profitable venture for us. Once again, we were made very welcome by everyone at the saleroom. And the bonus was that this was another charming historic town, very pretty, which made it a pleasure to visit.

The Bury St. Edmunds sale was conducted, as at Willingham, in two rooms simultaneously. There was furniture in one room - where I would buy, and in the other room there were smalls, collectables, jewellery, and pottery - where Cathy would buy at the same time. The saleroom was situated in the town centre, a few minutes from the large, colourful, and very busy outdoor market. As Cathy's business was usually finished before mine, she took the opportunity to go and explore, and always came back laden with fresh food and flowers.

Sometime later, Colin relinquished the premises in Saffron Walden. We had enjoyed many visits to this charming and pretty little town, and on one memorable occasion we were lucky enough to meet up with our daughter Alison for lunch, as she had recently moved to nearby Royston. Following the closing of Saffron Walden, Colin opened an additional saleroom at Willingham, and sometime after that he commenced a large re-building programme to further expand the auction facilities at the Willingham site.

The eyesight problem which had brought forward our southern explorations had been, in some ways, a blessing in disguise. We were grateful for the success of these trips, and we always enjoyed our weekends away. I was, however, always aware that the condition could resurface in the other eye - but I pushed that thought to the back of my mind.

Chapter 25
The Cotswolds Beckoned.

Following the death of our good friend and customer, Caroline, we continued to deal with her partner, Paul Richings. They had traded from several prestigious outlets, including The Swan at Tetsworth, and Station Mill Antiques at Chipping Norton. In Station Mill they had a large unit selling mainly antique pine, from where they had traded successfully for some twelve years prior to Caroline's death.

I knew from my conversations with Caroline and Paul that Station Mill had a very high footfall, and since it was only fifteen miles from Richard at Pine and Things in Shipston on Stour, it seemed a logical step to consider this as an outlet for us.

We did not require this as an outlet for pine, as we had many customers for that, but an additional outlet for the myriad of other interesting antiques we were now dealing in could be very useful, and hopefully financially rewarding. A bonus was that it would be very easy, and cost effective, to service a pitch at Station Mill when we made our regular deliveries to Richard.

Initial enquiries at the centre revealed a considerable waiting list of potential clients. However, with a good recommendation from Paul, April 2007 saw us through the doors of the centre - although initially we could only get rental space within a cabinet, which was £85 per calendar month. The cabinet was in an excellent position just inside the main entrance, but the most important benefit was that it got us higher up the waiting list for a proper floor-space unit. It took only a couple of months before we were offered a small pitch on the top floor.

On my first trip to place my furniture on the pitch, I was treated to a mild telling off. The manager deemed that I had overfilled the pitch, but I had the last laugh when a phone call from the centre a couple of hours later informed me that they had sold several of my items already, and all was well. We were off to a flying start.

Six weeks later, we were offered a much larger pitch, still upstairs but in an excellent trading position. We took it even though the rent was double.

In the meantime, Cathy had been selling on eBay and had achieved considerable success with porcelain and china, in particular dinner and tea services, which she had been trading in huge quantities. Her success with this encouraged us to expand our eBay activities into upholstered furniture, chaise longues, parlour suites, drop-end sofas, and the like.

We arranged delivery of the eBay sales whenever possible around our trips to Willingham and Bury St Edmunds; on one occasion delivering a drop-end sofa to a small terraced house in Wimbledon, where we only just got it through the door, and from there only got it into the sitting room by taking out the understairs cupboard – then through London back to Cambridge where we attended the sale at Willingham the next day, following an overnight stop.

Similarly, on another occasion, we delivered to Ramsgate, then with an overnight hotel stop returned to Cambridge via St Albans, where we made a second delivery on route, and attended the sale the next day. We certainly enjoyed a few good trips out and weekends away, with the delivery fee covering the cost of our overnight stops.

We also started to visit another old established auction room - Seth Jones in Wrexham, which was now run by his daughter and son-in-law. We found some bargains there for a while and enjoyed quite a few lunches from the Kentucky Fried Chicken which was next door! This saleroom sadly closed in 2008, when the family deemed that small salerooms like this were no longer viable - an ongoing trend I'm afraid.

We also ventured further into Wales, making regular visits to buy from Huw Williams in Porthmadog. We had gone to Porthmadog on our family holidays for about thirty years, and contact with Huw had become a regular feature of the holiday; once again I was able to combine business with pleasure (and profit). As our family grew up, we no longer holidayed in Porthmadog, but still travelled there to buy from Huw.

We had, by now, ceased standing at the Newark Fair. For us, it lacked the vibrancy that it once had. Also, when we had secured a floor unit at Station Mill in Chipping Norton, we vacated our space at GB Antiques in Lancaster - although it was a very popular outlet, for us it was time to move on.

In due course we secured a double pitch in a prime location on the ground floor within Station Mill. This was of great benefit to me as I had by now developed severe arthritis in both my knees, and carrying furniture upstairs was becoming a problem. Our sales continued to improve at Station Mill; we sold considerable amounts of the china and pottery that Cathy dealt in, particularly large dinner services, often selling two or three of these each week.

In the meantime, Clive from The Pine Merchant in Cambridge had sold his business and retired. He strongly recommended us to the new owner, and we were fortunate to secure uninterrupted and ongoing dealings with Birgit, the charming lady who had taken it on.

Also around this time, Richard at Pine and Things told me of his plans to emigrate to the USA, where his mother-in-law resided, and he too assured me that when he found someone to take over, he would recommend me to the new owners.

Although we were still supplying both of these outlets, the likelihood was that the amount we sold to each would be reduced. With this is in mind, and with the encouragement of Colin - the owner of Willingham auctions - we decided to enter more "finished pine" into his sale, something we had already been doing, but on a small scale.

This arrangement proved to be very satisfactory. While Cathy was bidding for pottery at the Willingham auction, the staff would unload the furniture from our van and book it in, ready for the following sale. They would get the furniture items listed, and then start loading our purchases from that day's sale - thus these were very profitable two-way trips.

During the summer months of 2009, I underwent keyhole surgery to repair the cartilage on each of my knees, with a promise that if not successful, knee replacements would follow. Each of these procedures involved a period of two weeks abstinence from travel, both before and afterwards. To keep the business alive, our sons David and Kevin took it in turns to drive Cathy to the Station Mill Centre at Chipping Norton, and then on to the saleroom at Willingham - unloading and replenishing stock at both places.

I would keep in touch with Station Mill by weekly phone calls, and on one particular Monday morning when I rang to check on my weekend sales, I was greeted with some unbelievable and shocking news; I was told that there had been a fire the evening before, the staff were still trying to contact all the dealers, and they were operating from a portacabin in the yard. The building had been almost completely destroyed, a large part of it was completely gutted and quite a few dealers had lost all their stock.

The extent of my losses was unclear at this stage. No one was allowed to enter the building, but I would be advised when it would be safe to go in and hopefully retrieve any salvageable stock. Some weeks later, when I was able to travel, David drove me down. We were permitted only a limited amount of time inside the building as it was considered unsafe, and hard hats were compulsory.

We were extremely fortunate. Apart from some minor water damage, most of my stock was saved, as my pitch was at the end of the building and quite a distance from the epicentre of the fire.

The future of Station Mill seemed at first to be uncertain, but Stephanie, the manager, gave regular updates. When it was decided that they were going to rebuild completely, I was assured that I would be allocated a similar selling position to where I had been before.

The rebuilding took almost a year, during which time I concentrated on selling goods through Willingham and, to a lesser extent, through Lacy Scott and Knight at Bury St Edmunds. I continued to do business with Pine and Things, and with The Orangery in Cambridge, which was the new name for The Pine Merchant, but with reduced quantities in both.

Whilst attending an auction at Willingham one day, I was not totally surprised to find my old friend Jack Robinson from Wigan in attendance. I had been going for ten years by this time and this was the first time Jack was there, but given the vast quantities of goods that he exported, it was inevitable that he would be looking to expand his buying opportunities. Jack was, at his peak, sending 120 containers every year to destinations all over the world, and he required large quantities of stock to fill them. I had first met Jack back around 1980, when one of his Japanese customers bought some goods from our shop and I delivered them to Wigan for packing.

Jack's setup was truly impressive and very, very different! He had purchased a lot of the old terraced properties around his warehouse, which was a former bakery. The terraced houses had then been demolished leaving a vast open area, where he had erected a large open-fronted storage building, adjacent to which was parked a long line of shipping containers.

Jack would stand at a kind of rostrum outside the building, where there was a steady stream of dealers bringing a wide range of antique goods to sell to him. As he purchased each item, Jack directed his staff by shouting out orders such as:

'This, this and this - container number one, bound for America.'
'This, this and this - container number three, bound for Japan.'
'This lot over here - container number seven, for Australia,' and so on.

On my first visit, I saw a mouth-watering quantity of good quality antique pine - just up my street - stacked outside the building. I anxiously enquired about buying. Jack told me politely but firmly that he sold all his pine to one dealer who took it all, and that it would be unethical for him to sell me any part of it. As I went on to find out, Jack was fiercely loyal to all his dealer associates and, although I got on very well with Jack, it was a many years before I was able to buy from him.

I would frequently meet Jack at the more local auction rooms, where we often enjoyed a cup of tea and a slice of cake together. On this first time of meeting at the Willingham sale, I was able to assure him that their on-site cafe was one of the best, and promptly went off to treat him to the first of many slices of cake that day.

With my local knowledge of the area, I was able to tell Jack of a short cut from the A14, which went through the pretty picture postcard villages, which he appreciated.

I introduced him to Lacy, Scott and Knight at Bury St. Edmunds, where I assured him that he would find a considerable quantity of goods suitable for his customers. This auction room did indeed serve him well, as he rarely bought less than two vanloads each time, and sometimes even more.

A couple of years later, I was saddened to learn from his son that Jack had suffered a stroke, and sadly was never again able to go on his long forays. In May 2020, my friend Paul Norris told me that Jack had died, but not of the coronavirus. Unfortunately, because of the lockdown measures in place, attendance at his funeral was limited. He was a popular and well-respected dealer and a rugby enthusiast. He was indeed another character who will be sadly missed.

To return to my story, back in 2010, with the rebuilding of Station Mill antique centre almost complete, I received a telephone call from Stephanie the manager informing me that due to management organisation, I would be allocated an area on the upper floor, rather than the ground floor as had been previously agreed.

This change of plan was entirely unacceptable to me, as during the ten months we had been waiting for the reopening of Station Mill, I had had one knee replacement operation and was on the short list for the second knee to be done in the very near future. The prospect of taking on an upstairs unit was out of the question, so I declined, and requested the refund of my deposit which they had been holding.

It was time for a rethink. Time to move on. Further adventures beckoned.

Chapter 26
Fate Intervenes.

Willingham Auctions had by now, March 2011, been a consistent destination for 10 years, and together with Lacy Scott and Knight had become the mainstay of our buying and selling for the past year.

Colin and Gale at Willingham were always very enthusiastic about our restored and refinished antique pine, and good prices were achieved for us there. They had expanded their cafe, which had originally only opened on sale days, into a thriving six days a week eatery. They had also developed a retail unit on the site for garden furniture etc. This meant that there was a steady footfall through the premises throughout the week. Items that had remained unsold in the auction were made available to purchase to the public at the reserve price, which meant that virtually everything we sent to Willingham was sold, one way or the other.

I was able to enter a wide variety of items with considerable success, and when Colin increased the frequency of the sales, from four weekly to every three weeks, we were kept busy supplying just this one outlet. Although we did sell well at Lacy Scott and Knight, we were never so successful in achieving high prices. We gradually dropped off with our visits there, and although we always intended to go back because we loved the "Olde Worlde" town of Bury St Edmunds, we never did.

Our overheads remained low - now with no rents for fairs or centres - but I was keen to try something else. Having all your eggs in one basket is never a good plan.

In past years, travelling to Lincolnshire whilst dealing with Colin Robinson and Barry Sykes and his sons, we had occasionally called into Hemswell Antique Centres, a large ex-RAF base with several antique centres on site.

We were very impressed with the main group of centres, which were in three separate buildings under the ownership of Robert Miller, and we had followed his development and expansions through news in the Antiques Trade Gazette.

With the decision not to return to the rebuilt Station Mill Antiques at Chipping Norton, and with ever-decreasing sales to the new owner at Pine and Things, I had the sudden urge in May 2011 to move into another antique centre. I have always believed that it is beneficial to sell in an area far away from where the items are bought, so that the stock presented is fresh to, and generally unseen by, potential clientele. Hemswell seemed the obvious choice.

Hemswell Antiques Centre, despite its size, rarely has vacancies. A call to the office confirmed none were available, but they would pass on my interest to the owner, Robert.

Robert did indeed call me a few days later and suggested that we visit the centres, and he would personally show us around. Cathy and I made the journey down the following day, and at the end of our tour Robert informed us of a forthcoming vacancy at the beginning of the next month in Building Two. Unfortunately, this unit was on the upper floor, and as I had had recent knee replacements, this was not ideal. However, Robert assured us that assistance would always be available to get our furniture up the stairs, and that he would move us to a downstairs unit when one became vacant.

We decided to take the plunge and moved into Building Two at the beginning of June 2011.

Cathy and I travelled down, accompanied by Pete Kelly, whose help with carrying our furniture up the stairs and setting out the stand was greatly appreciated. Sales seemed a little slow to begin with, as we had become accustomed to a very consistent number of sales every week at Station Mill. Maybe I was a bit impatient! However, when things did start moving, we found that we were able to sell more unusual and expensive items very well.

Occasionally I would take Pete with me, especially when there were any particularly heavy pieces. On one occasion, we took a very large table and a large mirror-backed sideboard, together with several other items which we set up on the pitch. Feeling very pleased with the display, we arrived back at Hill View around 3pm; just as we turned into our drive at home, I received a phone call from the staff at Building Two, advising me that a customer had bought all the large items already, so it was necessary to return the following week to restock!

In all, we had a very successful first year there, and continued to sell regularly at Willingham Auctions.

I began to revisit the fairs, beginning with the new one-day Swinderby Fair, and the Arthur Swallow two-day fair at Lincoln Showground. I quickly established contact with a few good dealers from whom to buy. It was also very easy to call into Hemswell Centre on the way back home and restock our stand there.

I did, however, begin to resent the fact that I had not been given the opportunity of a ground floor space, whilst noticing that new dealers were coming in and getting any available ground floor units when they became vacant. Although vacancies occurred infrequently, I assumed that Robert had forgotten my request. He knew that things were ticking over very well for me, and I know that he was always being pestered by others in the centre, as well as new dealers, for a "better" space.

Whatever the reason, one day I decided to give notice to leave - this was part way through my second year there. We were required to give a month's notice, and towards the end of the second week of my notice period, I received a call from Robert. He informed me that he was sorry I was leaving, and that in the future he would be glad to offer me a place in his latest expansion - he had bought "The Guardroom", a prominent building at the entrance to the site, which needed extensive renovation.

Robert's plan was to almost completely rebuild it and add an upper floor. It was to become his "flagship" building and he would be happy for me to be part of this new venture.

I explained my reasons for giving notice, but without hesitation I accepted his offer and added that, in that case, I would withdraw my notice to leave. Robert agreed and promised that I would have a ground floor space in his new building. He also invited me to become a member of the committee he was setting up to meet regularly and discuss the development of "The Guardroom".

Being on this committee was enjoyable and very interesting. We discussed the progress of this development, and were able to look around the site. We met every four or five weeks, had a tour around the developing building, and Robert would outline how the floor plan and fittings within the building (such as lighting and divisions between the stalls) would be implemented.

When all the building work had been carried out and the building opened, it was truly spectacular. It was, and is, an impressive addition to his other three buildings, showcasing the very best of antiques and deserving the definition of being the best in the country. Hemswell Antique Centre is the largest antique centre in Europe, and I am pleased to be a part of this.

During this time, I had remained in Building Two and did eventually get a ground floor pitch, which Robert had kindly arranged to have redecorated prior to my move there. As the building work on the Guardroom neared completion and the opening day approached, I was aware that Robert was under intense pressure from many dealers to be allocated prime positions there.

Diana, the designated manager, advised me after one of our committee meetings that I had been allocated a pitch on the upper floor. This was a large, imposing pitch in a great position but not the ground floor position which I had been promised. I decided not to take this pitch and remained in Building Two only.

Diana acted quickly and rang me the next day to say that she had negotiated a ground floor space, right opposite the counter, by the entrance, seemingly perfect. I could not have imagined a better spot. However, when the building did open, the reality was that my sales there were disappointing, so after four months I left the Guardroom and just continued in Building Two.

I decided to try selling at the bigger fairs again, after a gap of ten years. We booked a "shopping arcade" pitch at Arthur Swallow's Lincolnshire showground in August 2013, and my daughter Bernadette accompanied me on this occasion. I took a variety of stock and planned to stand for just one day, combining selling with buying from my usual sources - mainly to sell through Willingham auction. We had a fair degree of sales success and trade was generally busy, but it lacked the vibrancy of previous years. We booked a shopping arcade pitch again for the October of that year, but after a promising start with brisk sales, it began raining around 9am and then it teemed down all day long. The buyers simply disappeared.

I decided thereafter to take a different approach. Take a chance on the weather and book an outside stand at half the cost, taking just sufficient stock to cover our expenses regardless of the weather, but mainly using the pitch as an opportunity to be onsite early to buy from the other dealers there.

This new pitch was on the main avenue as buyers entered the fair, so was in a prime position. We discovered that our immediate neighbour was an old business contact, Barry Sykes, who had been living in France for some twenty years and now came over from France to sell French furniture at the fair. I had dealt with Barry and his sons over many years. It was nice to be next to an old friend, and we were able to help one another.

Sales at the fair, although not brilliant, were sufficient to cover all costs. We were able to buy from other dealers, and the fact that the fair was only ten miles from Hemswell Antique Centre meant that we could pop in and top up our stall there on the way home.

We always took our white German Shepherd, Georgie, with us. She loved going there, was as good as gold, sat quietly ignoring all the passing (often yapping) dogs, and attracted many admirers.

Another change that we witnessed at the Fairs was the now constant presence of TV companies filming programmes such as Bargain Hunt. These "new" antique-themed TV shows were becoming very popular and we knew most of the presenters – mostly due to crossing paths at the many different auction rooms we have attended in our years of dealing.

One of these auctions was Frank Marshall & Co. at Knutsford, and I regularly bought several lots there. On my first visit, when registering as a buyer, I met a young auctioneer called Adam Partridge. He prided himself in being a very fast auctioneer, which indeed he was.

One day I purchased a small set of pine drawers, which were in fact the end section of a pine dresser - these lovely Victorian items had been regularly butchered by later generations, who found them too large for modern homes and simply cut the end off! At the conclusion of the sale, Adam approached me and said, 'I've got two of those sets of pine drawers at home in my garage, are you interested?' I was.

On the viewing day of the next sale, Alan brought these items with him in the boot of his car. When I asked the price he said, 'Same as you paid last time, £10.' Deal done!! I guess that he wanted to avoid paying the commission if he had put them into the sale.

I continued to have a good rapport with Adam, and when he started doing a considerable amount of TV work (bargain hunt, flog-it, etc), I knew that he was destined for greater things. Indeed, he was. He later went on the establish his own auction rooms, first in Macclesfield, then Liverpool, and valuation offices at several other locations including Preston.

We had also regularly attended Clitheroe Auction Mart, where they traded the antiques under the title "Silverwood Auctions", thus differentiating it from the long-established livestock market at the same location. This antiques auction was developed with the guidance of Wilf Mould, who in earlier years had worked in Chorley for Smith & Hodkinson.

Wilf was a very good auctioneer with a non-nonsense approach. In later years, he also appeared quite often on TV programmes.

It was during one of my regular weekly visits to Clitheroe that I first met Danny Sebastian, known locally as "Seb", a colourful character who always wore a trilby hat – usually with a feather in it. We often competed for the same lots, but never with any bad feeling, in fact he was very jovial and always ready for a chat. His van stood out with equally flamboyant signwriting. It said something like: "follow me to beautiful things", but I can't remember exactly.

One day, whilst talking to Cathy and myself, Danny proudly opened the doors of his van to show how cosy it was inside. He explained that when travelling about, he could just jump in the back and, in his words, "have a kip".

Over time, I saw Danny at several auctions and antique fairs, and he too became involved in a considerable amount of TV work. He was a natural, and was just the same on-screen as when you met him in any other environment - always friendly and happy to chat and joke. I still occasionally see him around; he hasn't changed a bit, except that he has graduated to a rather faster set of wheels!

A final anecdote on the "wheel of fame and fortune" is Eric Knowles. We first met Eric at the NEC Antiques for Everyone Fair. Eric later set up a collector's club and we were members for a while, until it eventually fizzled out - but Eric certainly did not fizzle out! He has gone on to be one of the most recognised TV personalities in the antiques genre, and is still seen on many different shows to this day.

I continued dealing in much the same way (Hemswell, Willingham, Lincoln Fair etc) until, at the beginning of 2015, I decided to temporarily leave Hemswell - and have a rethink.

The fair continued, with Cathy accompanying me. I developed a good buying circle, and with the goods purchased there I achieved very good prices at Willingham Saleroom. Whilst at the fair, I did occasionally see Robert Miller - the owner of Hemswell antiques. He always said that he would be happy for me to return whenever I wanted. This had always been part of my plan, and we entered dialogue to find a suitable ground floor pitch.

And then fate played an unexpected hand.

In August 2016, Cathy and I celebrated our 50th wedding anniversary with our family. We rented a small holiday complex in Northumberland, complete with an indoor pool. Our daughter Alison and her husband Tom brought their dog, and we took Georgie - who again, loved it. We were there over the August Bank Holiday and returned home on the Monday evening. On Tuesday, I journeyed to Willingham with a van load of goods to enter into their next sale, and as usual was accompanied by Georgie. The journey there and the delivery of the goods went smoothly. The return journey proved to be anything but smooth!!

My usual route home would be via the A14 and the M6, but due to long delays around Birmingham I diverted to the M42 and M40 to link up with the M5, and then re-join the M6 further north. As I approached the junction of the M5 from the M40, I suddenly realised that the power steering had ceased to function, and there appeared on the dashboard an alarming array of warning lights.

I decided to endeavour to reach the north-bound services on the M5, hoping that I would make it safely there, and then call for assistance. Some fifteen minutes later I successfully arrived, pulled into the services, and stopped at the first available parking area - which was the coach park. A quick check under the bonnet confirmed my suspicion that the fanbelt had snapped and bent the lower pulley wheel. A call to my breakdown company confirmed that they would have a technician with me within the hour. This later extended to one and a half hours, and when he did eventually arrive, he simply said that he needed to arrange a transporter to continue my journey home.

He issued the necessary paperwork to enable me to extend the free parking time on the services, and then he was gone!

As I was unsure how long I would be waiting for the transporter and as such I was reluctant to leave my vehicle to get anything to eat, so I spent the time sitting with Georgie in the back of the van with the doors wide open - fortunately it was a lovely warm and sunny day. Georgie was well catered for, as I always travelled with plenty of water and a spare can of food for her.

I found it necessary on that day to wear my dark sunglasses the whole time. After the loss of sight in my right eye sixteen years earlier, I had experienced extreme "light sensitivity".

I was forced to ring the breakdown service several more times that afternoon, until eventually I spoke to someone who was extremely concerned about the length of time that I had been waiting, and promised me that he would not leave his shift until he was assured that I had been rescued.

He was as good as his word and rang me several times over the next few hours until eventually, around 8pm, a transporter finally arrived. By this time, I had been stranded for about eight hours and it was starting to go dark.

The driver loaded my vehicle, but Georgie was forced to remain in the back of the van as dogs were not allowed to travel in the cab of the transporter. We finally arrived home at about 11.30pm - my drama having started around midday. I had set off that morning at 4.30am.

We offered to put the driver up for the night, but he explained that he needed to get on his way. The following day we managed to get the van to our local garage where it was repaired, and then it was returned to us the day after that, which was Thursday.

By now, the uncomfortable sensation in my eyes that had started while waiting on the motorway services was worsening – and it seemed to be worsening in my "good" eye. I made an appointment with my optician, which was arranged for the Saturday morning. Cathy took me to this appointment, and although it was initially determined that I needed stronger distance glasses, the optician decided to do additional tests involving stronger drops - after which she became concerned, and referred me immediately to the eye specialist at Royal Preston Hospital.

The specialist who examined me was familiar with the condition which had affected my left eye some sixteen years previously - Anterior Ischaemic Optic Neuropathy. Within ten minutes he was able to tell me that this same condition had now affected the other eye. And that it was no longer safe for me to drive.

So, from the second Saturday of September 2016 I had to cease driving, knowing that this was indeed life changing. I was no longer independent, and my time of dealing in antiques was looking like coming to an abrupt end.

Chapter 27
All Change.

Following this initial diagnosis, I had regular hospital consultations and tests with eye specialists over the next few months, culminating in being officially registered as "Sight Impaired" in 2017.

Following that news, I was seen immediately by a specialist nurse, who gave me excellent advice and support, and guidance on how to proceed. Her advice was to try to develop my interests around the condition, and carry on doing as much as possible of my normal life. It was clear that they were concerned about the effects of how such devastating news could affect you mentally. Accept the change and adapt was the clear message.

Having enquired about my occupation, or indeed if I was still working, the nurse advised that I endeavour to carry on, if that was what I enjoyed doing. I was furnished with leaflets giving me information about where to obtain support by organisations such as Galloways and the Royal National Institute for the Blind (RNIB).

I think it is fair to say that I did accept the change as inevitable, and decided to look forward rather than back. I think my focus at that time was the idea of getting a guide dog, which as a lifelong dog-lover, was definitely a positive prospect.

Our middle daughter Alison very quickly arranged a visit from the Guide Dogs for the Blind organisation. This was a very positive visit. They assured me that I was certainly eligible for a guide dog, and they would add my name to the waiting list, but there were reservations because of where we lived. Our house fronted onto an unlit country road, which was very busy with heavy traffic using it as a shortcut from the A59 to Leyland, and there was no footpath along the road near the house. This would be a dangerous situation for both me and the guide dog.

This began the thought process of having to move.

Changes to my life inevitably meant change for Cathy also, especially if I was to continue antique dealing. She decided that the extremely long distance travelling which I had always done, with a large fully laden van, would be extremely challenging for her. However, she happily managed pickups and deliveries within a thirty mile radius using either the van or my large estate car, and so I was able to continue buying and selling and enjoying life.

Willingham Auctions were also very flexible by permitting deliveries of my goods to them on Saturdays, when my friend Peter Kelly was available. This allowed that important part of my business to continue.

During this time, I had commenced training to use the "long cane" (the white stick) to enable me to walk independently. Again, this was impossible to do near to our house, so the instructor drove me to the local villages and towns for this.

We knew without doubt that we would have to move - a big wrench after thirty-seven years in our beloved home, Hill View.

We instructed the estate agents, and our property was placed on the market in August 2017. There was a steady flow of viewings, at least one a week, but no serious offers were made until almost Christmas. When we had two!!

From the outset of marketing our house we set about decluttering thirty-seven years of accumulation, including our large barns which were full.

Our son David came from his home in Sheffield as often as possible at weekends, and many trips were made to the tip and charity shops, not to mention weekly trips to Warren and Wignalls with goods to auction. It was of course not just the contents of the house - we had three very large out-buildings which contained literally decades of accumulated "treasure". Once we had received our first firm offer, the work to downsize intensified.

David then came to help us every weekend from the start of 2018. Our first offer on the house fell through, but the second went through successfully and when, around June 2018, we knew that our sale was looking definite, it became urgently apparent that we had to find a new home.

Our original intention was to move into the village of Longton, where there are some lovely properties, and although there were lots on the market, nothing appealed to me other than a bungalow at Bank Croft. This appeared to offer potential but had been empty for some time and was in poor condition with subsidence, so we dismissed this.

Cathy searched the internet daily, and we made daily excursions to view externally. I dismissed them all. Cathy was becoming increasing impatient, constantly suggesting properties to view, and getting no enthusiasm from me.

She widened the search to outside Longton.

When she suggested Leyland, I immediately refused, remembering the unpleasantness caused by our neighbours at Edinburgh Close almost forty years earlier. After further frustrating internet searching, she found a property which had come on the market only that day, and which sounded promising. She loved it, and she knew immediately that this was the one for us. But when she told me that it was in Leyland, my immediate response was 'No, No, NO!'

After a few moments, in which she expressed her utter frustration, I tentatively asked 'Where abouts in Leyland?' 'Parkgate Drive' was her answer. I hesitated.

I remembered Parkgate Drive from my days working for Unigate, and I knew that it was close to Worden Park. The sale of Hill View was progressing, and by now it was a matter of urgency to find a new home.

We decided to drive to Leyland and do a quick assessment of the area. We both liked the look of the house in Parkgate Drive; it was a chalet bungalow and just perfect for us, in a pretty street, backing on to woodland and a park, near to shops and all the amenities of town, including bus stops! It had been thirty-seven years since we had lived close to a bus stop, but actually this might well become very important to us, given my sight loss and our advancing years.

We arranged a viewing for the next day. We both knew, without doubt, that we had found our future home. We made an offer, negotiated, and had an acceptance the following day. All settled within three days, and under a week since this property had gone on the market. There was no onward chain. We completed within six weeks and moved in on 24th August 2018.

Without doubt, we always seem to know when a property is the right one for us, and I have been fortunate that making decisions of this magnitude have been incredibly easy. I just seem to know when it is right... when it is "meant to be".

With the house decided on, a month before we moved, I took a pitch in Preston Antique Centre (aka "The Mill") some thirty years since I was last a stallholder there. This would give me a base to work from - and a home for some of my surplus furniture. I enjoyed being back in The Mill, making several new acquaintances and renewing old ones.

I continued trading, mainly in antique pine, using our son Kevin's workshop in Bold Street Preston for preparation work - selling some items at Preston Antique Centre, and taking a batch every month to Willingham Auctions (with someone else driving of course!).

In early 2019, I gradually began to do less pine furniture and diversified even further into other areas of antiques, especially unusual and rare items. I honed my years of experience to now buy what *I liked*, without the urgency to "turn things over".

In May 2019, I took the decision to apply to Hemswell Antiques Centre again, with my son David's help. Conversations with Robert Miller, owner of Hemswell, confirmed that he would likely have a space for us - either in Building One or the Guardroom, both considered prestige sites.

David and I combined a trip to the "new" Newark One-Day Fair with a visit to Hemswell Antique Centre. After a brief tour with Robert, we decided on a smallish pitch which was on the upper floor of the Guardroom, where we were welcomed back by Diana, the ever efficient, hardworking, and charming manager of the Guardroom.

Our moving in date was given as the 1st of June 2019.

I hired a van for three days. My sons David and Kevin took me to the Newark two-day fair which was on the Thursday and Friday of that week. My sons now acted not only as my chauffeur, but also as "my eyes", guiding me around the fair to avoid falls, and advising me of the condition of any prospective purchases.

Their muttered words (and sometimes alarmed cries) of 'No dad… too much damage, too much woodworm' and so on, rang out around that fair many times.

We returned to Leyland, unloaded our purchases, reloaded the van with the goods to go to fill the new pitch at Hemswell, and all was set for the trip there on the following day, Saturday - this time with Pete Kelly roped in to do the chauffeuring.

At least, that was the plan!!!

However, around teatime on the Friday evening Cathy became very unwell, resulting in an exciting trip in an ambulance, and emergency admission to hospital. As soon as I realised the seriousness of the situation, I knew that I could not make the trip to Hemswell the next morning. I rang Kevin and he agreed to travel down with Pete to do the set up the next day.

Our daughter Bernadette accompanied me to the hospital, where we spent an anxious few hours in A and E. Once Cathy's condition was stabilised and she was admitted to a ward, we returned home. It was now 4am. Fortunately Cathy's condition improved, and a week later she was back home and on her way to recovering.

So, the set-up to our new venture began without me!!!

The boys met up at Hemswell with David, who travelled there separately from his home in Sheffield. They did a good job of getting everything in place, and, in fact, made our first sale that afternoon. Sales remained steady, and we expanded our selling space, first with a cabinet for collectables, and later with a second pitch, giving us extra floor space.

In the meantime, having decided (after fifty-plus years) to finally stop dealing in stripped pine furniture, I relinquished my space in Preston Antique Centre at the end of August 2019 - with the view that, health permitting, I would return with a different selection of stock to sell.

We took on the second pitch in Hemswell in March 2020, just prior to the closure of the centre due to the Covid-19 pandemic. Internet sales continued online thanks to the hard work of Robert Miller and his team, and I secured the services of a courier to facilitate the delivery of goods to the centre during lockdown. The partial reopening in the summer 2020 permitted a direct visit by myself, with Kevin and Pete's assistance, to restock and reorganise.

From the 1st November 2020, I took on yet more space at Hemswell, this time in Building One. Throughout the shutdown, I continued to service all my stands there. With the help of the courier and the hard work of all the staff at Hemswell, sales continued via the internet.

Chapter 28
Still adapting.

With the start of 2021 and our new stand in Hemswell came an increase in covid, and a further lockdown.

It was to be some six months before I was finally able to visit our new pitch in Building One with assistance from my son in law, Pete Nickson (Maggie's husband). There had been encouraging sales and I was pleased with progress despite the lockdowns; Hemswell had good online presence and sales through this medium were better than I had expected.

I had kept in touch with my old friend Paul Norris throughout the covid pandemic and indeed he had occasionally moved items in his van for me, such as purchases from a couple of different salerooms. Paul suggested that one day he might like to return to Preston Antique Centre. He had semi-retired two years earlier, but was considering returning if he could share a pitch with someone, and hence keep expenses to a minimum. We decided to jointly apply to Sue Shalloe, who runs "The Mill", and were given a very good stand on the ground floor - right opposite the office. We moved back in on July 1st, 2021.

Having ceased dealing in the antique pine for which I was so well known, sales were a little slow for me to begin with whilst I tried different items of stock. The antique business, like many others, does not stand still, and it is affected by fashions and trends, as well as availability.

The focus in recent years has been less about function, and more about the decorative appeal of an object. We used to sell tables and chairs, wardrobes, and chests of drawers - nowadays you are more likely to achieve a sale from something that has "the right look" or "the right colour" or is "upcycled". This is what has always made this trade interesting and kept dealers on their toes.

Preston Antique Centre has always been a hub for the trade, an enjoyable place to do business, bringing me into contact with dealers both old and new. It is also a place where I can buy stock occasionally, to supply my outlets elsewhere.

A year after Paul and I moved back into the centre, we found ourselves in a situation which made both of us decide, reluctantly, to leave this centre again at the end of August 2022. In my case, this was precipitated by a decline in the health of my wife Cathy. She and I have worked together in this business over the course of five decades. Her role in recent years has been the technological side of things such as the internet and email. She continued, as she always had, observing trends in what sells and the market direction in general.

Sadly, as we finally bring these memoirs to print, Cathy lost her struggle on 4th September 2022, and passed away in my arms as we (Kevin, his partner Sharon, and I) tried to get her back to hospital.

I received many messages from fellow dealers, who knew and liked her as a warm and friendly face wherever we went. Her loss to me is totally devastating. She wasn't just a huge part of my life; she was my life.

We all know that at some time the end is inevitable, but that makes it no easier to bear. I have frequently considered whether I should now give up the business of antique dealing, but as usual I have thought about what Cathy would say about that. When looking to buy items, it is not difficult for me to recognise things that she would like. I just ask myself 'Would Cathy like it?' If the answer is yes, I buy it.

In a way, continuing in the business keeps me close to her. And so, for now, with the help of others, I will continue. The staff at Hemswell, Sue Shalloe and staff at Preston Antiques Centre, all at Warren and Wignalls, my fellow dealers, and my family make this possible.

To find stock, I am increasingly dependent on David and Kevin, our two eldest sons, and my old friend Pete Kelly and my son in law Peter Nickson, who frequently transport me to the fairs, centres, and auction houses. Alison, her husband Tom and 5-year-old daughter Beatrix will take me to Hemswell and then on the big fair at Newark this week. I also need others' eyes to examine the finer details of the condition before I make a purchase. I know what I want to buy - and they check it out before I make an offer. Hopefully I shall continue in Hemswell for a while yet, but the days when I would leave home at 4am to travel to Cambridge then Windsor then Southampton then home again, six hundred miles and twenty hours later, are long gone.

I enjoy the search for new treasures, the banter and camaraderie of fellow dealers, and the shared passion that this brings. You always have the urge to continue - and so, I do.
With help and support from my family, particularly Bernadette and Maggie who have been excellent and patient teachers, I have even learned to use email and the internet.

When we began, antique stripped pine was the fashion. Today, the younger generation are into Scandinavian design, and G-plan and Ercol from the 1960s. Sustainability is a very important concern these days so repurposing and reusing antique furniture certainly has its place in today's world and going forward. There is now a great acceptance of mix and match of old and new, so this business has a great future.

As Buzz Lightyear says in Toy Story… 'To Infinity, and Beyond!'

Appendix – some photos

The early days starting out as a dealer! Everyone had a roof rack on their car.

Cathy and I at our wedding in 1966

A year later at my cousin Ann's wedding, Cathy is expecting David. My mother is sat to my right and my dad is the shorter man stood behind.

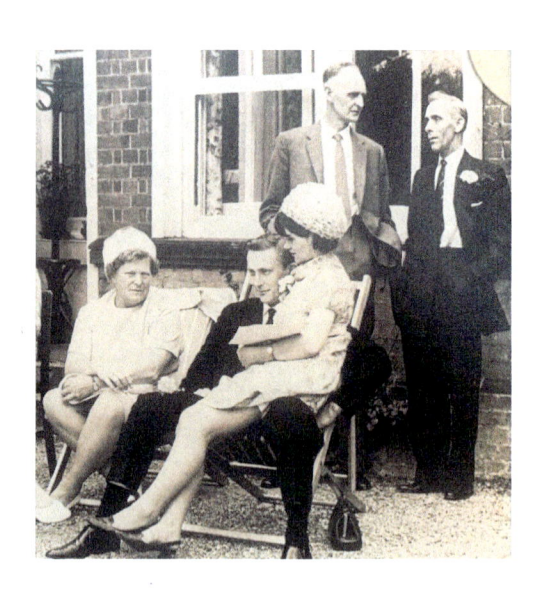

To sell or to sit? An antique dealer's dilema.
A fine East European settle.

A fine 19th centruy pine table, ready for delivery.
The photo shows our sheep in the background.
Approx. 1992 at Hill View

A Victorian small chest of drawers.
A favourite of the French market

A 19th century stripped pine chest of five drawers.
A typical example of thousands we sold – in particular to the American market.

A photograph kindly supplied by one of our customers.
The Old English Pine Company of St. Louis, USA.
Showing a selection of antique pine furniture supplied by us over several years.
With thanks to Alan and Pat Richardson

A photo of Penny Farthing Antiques, London, 1989.

Stock at our second shop in New Hall Lane
1992

A large selection of stock prepared for sale in our 'big shed' at Hill View.
May 1997

A selection of Victorian furniture "in the paint" before restoration.
May 1995

A selection of Victorian furniture, some before restoration.
October 1995

A lovely Scottish pine dresser, prepared for sale.
It is hard to find good "all-scots" pine examples.
July 1995

A good large pine kitchen table for the USA market.
August 1995.

The family in 2014 at Alison's wedding, back in the area around Portmadoc which had become very special for all the children.
Left to right – Stephen, Maggie, Bernadette, Alison, Cathy, me, David (jr) and Kevin.

The extended family with partners and grandchildren

173

'BURGLARS! NOT ON MY WATCH!'
This is Zodie - one of the many family dogs who were a part of the journey.
1998

Every Antiques' dealer has to own a Range Rover at least once in their lives!
With dogs Zita and Zodie in the grounds of our home for 37 years, Hill View. 1998.

My much beloved white German shepherd, Georgie, again in North Wales

The adventures continue….photos taken at my Guardroom stand at Hemswell Antiques Centre, freshly stocked with purchases made at Newark Antiques Fair that day

Taken in August 2023 - a week before my 80th birthday

10,000 ×25   250,000
  100,000   25,000

Printed in Great Britain
by Amazon